You Teach the Machines

AI On Your Terms

You Teach the Machines

AI On Your Terms

Jeff Pennington

Published by Balacynwood LLC, Philadelphia

First edition

Hardcover ISBN: 979-8-9988152-1-8
Softcover ISBN: 979-8-9988152-0-1
Ebook ISBN: 979-8-9988152-2-5
Audio Book ISBN: 979-8-9988152-3-2

Cover Designer Byron O'Neil
Photograph provided by author

Dedicated to my wife, Melissa Pennington,
whose love and support are apparently limitless.

Contents

PREFACE

"A book about AI? Are you using AI?"

"Ha, ha. No."

I always gave the same answer to the inevitable question asked by friends and colleagues who'd heard I left my job to write this book. But the reason changed over time.

At first, I refused to use AI because I didn't want to give my ideas and words away. That's what happens when you put your intellectual property into ChatGPT, Claude, all of them.

Then I refused to use AI because I wanted to do an experiment: write, edit, revise, and finalize the best Introduction I possibly could, then compare my work to an AI-edited version of my earliest, roughest first draft. See what the machine would do differently. Look for the results of this experiment at the end of the book.

Ultimately, I found so much joy, peace, and satisfaction in writing amongst the books of my local library that I stopped thinking about using AI. Looking up from my computer, I would let my eyes and mind wander over the titles on the shelves on either side of me. My mind and mood were lifted day after day when a random book inspired my narrative or sent me off researching a supporting argument. I was in what athletes call the "Zone." Putting ideas on the page became effortless. Hours flew by, and before I knew it, the winter sun had set and the kind librarians told me it was closing time.

I didn't use AI to write this book because I was having too much fun learning, thinking, and creating something to help the people I care about. Because I teach the machines. So can you.

INTRODUCTION

Like billions of people around the world, you may have suddenly become familiar with the following words straight out of Silicon Valley or a futuristic movie: Machine learning. GenAI. Large Language Model. Generative. Training. GPT. Explainability. Neural Network. Deep Learning. Hallucination.

These words are synonymous with Artificial Intelligence (AI), the computer systems we can teach to do "thinking" work. Sometimes we teach machines to find patterns of information that we can't, given the flood of data in our digital lives. Sometimes we teach machines to do a specific task in a way that augments our life or supports the work that we already do. The words above are casually thrown around by everyone from tech bros to journalists to advertisers to the AI "assistants" that are starting to pop up on every app and website. But they can distract from what is really going on.

You've picked up this book because "AI" seemingly comes up in every job interview, work meeting, or classroom discussion, shows up in every search you do online, invades your social media, and is splashed across every advertisement you see. And this all seems to have happened overnight. What changed? Everything. And nothing at all. Everything because we, as a digital society, have reached a tipping point. Nothing at all because for twenty years AI has been with us, becoming more and more capable behind the scenes. Is this scary? Exciting? What exactly is AI, anyway? You are likely thinking: How is "the machine" already in my life without me being aware? How do I make the most of the most important innovation since we humans first wrote things down 5,000 years ago and then, 575 years ago, figured out how to print copies? How do I protect myself, the people I care about, my education, and my job?

The truth is that you—and me, our parents, our kids—have been "teaching the machine" for years. We are all simultaneously consumers *and* producers in an AI economy that has been around for decades. This book is titled *You Teach the Machines* because it is fundamentally that simple. AI depends on *you*. The machine learns from the data you create, just as an infant learns the basics of language from the words you speak. The machine learns to do things that matter to you when you tell it right from wrong, just as a toddler learns grammar when you correct them.

Many corporations have much to gain from AI appearing to be Oz the Great and Powerful. Something magical, an otherworldly black box. It's not. It's just a machine, often with a cynical man behind the curtain—a machine taught with your data and your feedback. The more we all understand AI for what it is, the more we can maximize benefit and minimize harm. You've been teaching AI for as long as you've been using Google, Amazon, social media, and navigation apps, for as long as you've been going to the doctor and swiping your credit card. It's time to take charge and put AI to work for you. You teach the machines.

I started my tech career in 1996 during another period of rapid change. The web was brand new and data, for the first time, was considered an asset with a dollar value (Kerr, 1991). A few years on,

I started working in AI at Ask Jeeves, the first natural language internet search engine. Twenty-five years later, I created a comprehensive data asset and AI program as the Chief Research Informatics Officer of a leading pediatric academic medical center. I left that job, one I loved, to write this book. To help all of us navigate the change of AI.

If you, like most people, have a lot of questions, reservations, and even fears about AI, this book aims to demystify this groundbreaking technology and put your mind at ease. The chapters here will answer your questions about AI, including:

1. How did AI seemingly show up everywhere overnight?
2. What could change in my life because of AI?
3. Can I trust AI?
4. How do I use AI to make my life and my family's life better?

Cuneiform To ChatGPT

Your questions are, for the most part, about *change*. Change from the old normal is always accompanied by uncertainty, and we as humans are hardwired to fear what we don't know. Artificial intelligence is a relatively recent arrival in human history. We don't yet share a widespread understanding of AI or a new normal of daily use. Our uncertainty and fear are entirely natural and understandable. This is revolutionary technology!

Fundamentally, AI is a completely new way that we humans capture our knowledge. That hasn't happened since the Sumerians invented writing in ancient Mesopotamia around 3200 BC and people no longer had to simply remember everything. Historians think the first writing, called cuneiform, was invented to give a customer a grocery receipt. Before cuneiform writing, the only way to capture information was for one person to *remember* what another person *told them.* That meant there was no written history. No written receipts. No written recipes. Imagine you figured out that leaving open jars of barley out in a rainstorm made beer, another Mesopotamian innovation from roughly the same time. You tell the recipe to your friend over a few beers, but after a few too many, you both forget what it was. Fast forward to a time when cuneiform writing has been invented, and you happen upon the barley-in-the-rain trick again. This time, you write it down, and it gets passed along to generations thereafter. From that point forward, it was possible to record human knowledge, leading to massive cultural changes and advancements. Writing made it possible for individual humans to record important knowledge and share it with relatively few other humans (Finkel & Taylor, 2015). AI makes it possible for us to collect massive amounts of digital knowledge to share with others worldwide, like ChatGPT, which incredibly incorporates information scraped from a public archive of all the websites ever made called Common Crawl.

Artificial intelligence is also an entirely novel way to broadly share, disseminate, and use human knowledge. This hasn't happened with such seismic consequences since serial entrepreneur Johannes Gutenberg figured out how to scale up book production with moveable type in Mainz, Germany in 1450. Gutenberg borrowed heavily to do the R&D and engineering required to invent the printing press. His first book? Copies of the twenty-eight-page learn-to-read Latin schoolbook *Ars minor*, the first part of an ancient text called *Ars grammatica.* He's more famous for the next book he printed, the Bible, but it's notable that he started with an educational book, whether he did it intentionally or otherwise. In those days, you had to know Latin to get what might today be called an office job. Before Gutenberg, getting your kid started on *Ars grammatica* meant paying a scribe much of a laborer's yearly wage to hand-write a copy with pen and ink. That meant only better-off kids learned Latin and went to school. Whatever Johannes Gutenberg intended, printing relatively cheap copies of the equivalent of Dick and Jane for Latin was an early example of doing right by doing well. The cheaper it was to learn to read, the more books he could sell!

Eventually, a diaspora of trained printers who stole Gutenberg's technology set off an explosion of printing across Europe. A mere fifty years later, more than twelve and a half *million* books had been printed! Printing made it possible for a single human to record important knowledge, then share it with millions of others so they could do stuff with the knowledge. This invention, more than any other, launched Europe, and then the rest of the world, into the modern era. This shifting of the Earth is known as the *Gutenberg Effect*.

It's important to note that at the time, there was pushback against the printing press. Turns out the intellectual and ruling classes felt more secure when knowledge was captured and made available at great expense by scribes copying out books by hand. Secure in their stations, the ruling class viewed the work of a scribe as morally superior to the ink-stained labor of setting type and cranking a press. Classist snobbery was also fueled by the fact that the labor of printing was taken up by the lower classes. But the expansion of literacy in these same craftsmen, indentured apprentices, and servants opened new markets for popular books very different from highbrow manuscripts (Houston, 2016). For example, Desiderius Erasmus' widely read and sometimes-banned books advocated the then-radical idea that the church and monarchs should serve the people first (Erasmus, 1515; Erasmus, 1516).

Newspapers, magazines, radio, television, and the internet all extended the innovation of the printed book. All were initially disparaged. If you're of a similar vintage to me, you may remember some professors prohibiting the use of the internet to do research for your term paper. Be thoughtful about similar criticisms by today's intellectual elite as AI emerges and evolves. Know that some criticism of AI as somehow inauthentic may be in defense of the established cultural clout of experts. But also don't completely disregard these same experts, who are justifiably nervous. Some of their criticisms are valid, such as the potential for the erosion of critical thinking and writing skills due to the overuse of language AI.

How does AI relate to writing in ancient Mesopotamia and printing in medieval Germany? Historical, disruptive—and ultimately constructive—precedents of writing and printing help us understand changes in our lives caused by the emergence of AI. For now, consider that writing and then printing made it possible for the expertise, knowledge, and thoughts of a single human to spread through literacy and education to many other humans. At its worst, this can lead to Adolf Hitler's *Mein Kampf*. At its best, it can lead to Henry Gray's groundbreaking textbook *Gray's Anatomy*. Artificial intelligence can make it possible for human knowledge and expertise to spread even further, not just through other humans, but through machines we teach to augment our lives. Artificial intelligence makes it possible for us to capture the knowledge of many, many (all?) humans and share it so it can be used by many, many more (all?). But just as the printing press amplified whatever you printed with it, AI can amplify whatever we teach it. Sometimes for the worse, such as in 2023, when hackers who couldn't write computer code themselves used AI to generate code that they then used to attack an email company. Sometimes for the better when, the same year, biomedical researchers who couldn't write computer code themselves used the same AI to generate computer code at a prestigious hospital to get important data out of a database, greatly speeding up their important work. For better or worse, you teach the machines.

We started with a discussion of writing and printing, historical precedents of innovation that sparked massive global change, very deliberately because AI burst into our world through the exact same door: language.

Our Black Swan Moment

On November 30, 2022, a startup company called OpenAI released ChatGPT, an AI language tool that quickly gained widespread notoriety. The public reaction and significant notoriety of this tool in our public consciousness was an *outlier*, impossible to predict beforehand. There was a huge *impact* from this notoriety: its release and the subsequent freak-out in almost every corner of our society changed our conversations and expectations in a very big way, whether or not we actually took the time to play around with ChatGPT. Since that moment, we've been furiously working *after* the fact to explain how this all happened. We want to go back and figure out how we could have predicted how ChatGPT has upended our lives if we'd only paid attention. This trifecta of an *outlier* event with a huge *impact* we desperately try to *explain afterward* is characteristic of what's become known as a *black swan event.*

The Black Swan is a theory for understanding the outsized impact of rare events on human society. Events like the September 11 attacks and the subsequent public, political, and military response. It was highly improbable but changed everything (Taleb, 2007). A black swan event is also a matter of perspective. A number of expert analysts were not surprised by the attacks on September 11; to them an attack was certain, even if they did not know exactly when or where it would happen. The general public, the military, and much of the Federal government not only did not anticipate the attacks but were completely unprepared to handle such an improbable but consequential event. My goal in writing this book is to help you be informed so you may better handle the changes we can anticipate, especially the unlikely but consequential disruption AI is certain to cause. The more you know about AI, the more you use AI, the better off you will be in coping with unexpected events AI will bring in the future. Artificial intelligence depends on you. You teach the machines.

Sam Altman, CEO of OpenAI, may or may not have predicted the public reaction to his launch-and-see-what-happens "creative disruption." It's a typical path in the technology industry, both useful (gather new information) and intellectually lazy (skip the deliberation). Sam did it with his one and only startup before realizing investors (not entrepreneurs) made the big bucks, and he made enough money investing to convince him he was a Master of the Universe. Except his only prior startup was a failed social network app called Loopt. Lower stakes. He was successful enough as an investor to co-found OpenAI as a nonprofit artificial intelligence research organization that quickly evolved to have multiple for-profit subsidiaries. It's complicated. After launching ChatGPT, Sam claimed the release was a benevolent attempt to help us all face the reality of the new power of AI. That may or may not have been a reason. More likely it was to grab market share with a product built using an algorithm developed at Google and a few billion dollars he needed to show a return on.

Meanwhile, people at Google, including Geoffrey Hinton, one of the originators of modern AI, were doing the more difficult "just because we can, should we?" deliberation, carefully considering the implications of technology certain to cause major disruption. Ultimately, it doesn't matter what Sam claimed as his reason. The immediate impact on public discourse and industry was huge and will likely be viewed as historically significant.

The black swan of AI bursting into our consciousness made us feel like the world shifted underneath us. Professionally, I found myself in the middle of a storm of uncertainty and fear. My colleagues at the Children's Hospital of Philadelphia and I were stunned that ChatGPT had been put into the wild. We were hit by the black swan and found ourselves in the role of helping people who hadn't seen it coming to process and understand what had happened. All of a sudden, much of my job became explaining the emergence of AI after the fact. Before ChatGPT, our society didn't know that AI was around the corner. Now, we feel like we don't know what AI will bring, good or bad. The reality is that AI will almost certainly bring more black swan events in the future. But you also have more agency than you realize. You teach the machines.

Why is it worth considering our reaction to AI in the black swan context? Step back from AI for a moment. The black swan way of thinking is useful because it's about admitting we don't know what we don't know. The black swan theory says that randomness is more prevalent than we as humans are wired to accept. Many, if not most, of the truly important events in our lives or our society are unpredictable. So maybe—just maybe—we should balance the amount of time we try to predict and plan with more time spent preparing for change and uncertainty.

Please don't take this suggestion as a forecast for doom and gloom. We humans seem to be hardwired to see change and uncertainty as inherently bad, probably because we don't live very long, and we have evolved to be almost entirely concerned with self-preservation, and to see anything new as a threat. The emergence of

AI was jarring in the sensational way that it quickly went from tech company back office to dining room table conversation. We consider the idea of the black swan theory not so much because it explains the emergence of AI, but because it's a good way to prepare for the uncertainty that lies ahead—the certain-to-happen but impossible to predict unintended outcomes of AI. The black swan theory tells us it's up to us to work together to demand and take an active role in this change. So let's go back to the moment when ChatGPT burst onto the scene. Why did it seem like such a big deal?

ChatGPT delivered to everyday users a compelling language-based conversation experience on just about any topic. Note the use of the word "compelling" instead of "accurate" or "correct." This is an important point that we'll get back to. Over the next few months, social media, TV news, and traditional media exploded with examples of ChatGPT answering questions, writing poems, drafting letters, and summarizing information. We were seeing a credible artificial general intelligence application for the first time. ChatGPT is one among many examples of a "chatbot," a computer system taught to respond to text or voice. Chatbots had been mostly annoying and useless up until this point. Boomers, Gen Xers, and Millennials: Remember Clippy? Most recent chatbots weren't much better. They were rarely welcome, mostly unhelpful interjections to already painful customer service experiences. If it seemed like every chatbot you interacted with before ChatGPT was narrow-minded and knew nothing about your specific problem, you're right. Chatbots prior to the current generation were not much more than a fancy search interface to whatever narrow catalog of information their owner wanted you to go through before passing you on to a more expensive human. What was different this time?

The release of ChatGPT gave anyone who signed up for a free account an interface to incredibly powerful new language-based AI technology. Millions upon millions of people did just that and had their first experience with AI in a message-based conversational format that seemed to respond somewhat credibly on any topic. ChatGPT differed from our experience with Clippy and its chatbot descendants in part due to the many billions of dollars invested in its underlying "brain," a type of AI known as a "large language model" that we'll learn more about later. Suffice it to say, ChatGPT could reply to you more authentically based on its having read hundreds of millions of publicly available texts multiple times.

ChatGPT also used a new type of AI (more on this in just a bit) that was much better at figuring out the important words and phrases in your message. Prior chatbots were clumsier and not as insightful. People got super excited because ChatGPT seemed more responsive to what was important in their message. In a way, ChatGPT was the first chatbot that seemed like a good listener. And it could respond to questions on just about any topic because it had read just about everything on the internet. Did you know that ChatGPT was taught with the contents of every web page published all the way back to 2008? That includes but is not limited to every word written by copywriters in online clothing catalogs, every public website, and every online news article not behind a paywall. This was the closest we, the general public, had come to the artificial intelligence of popular science fiction.

Amara's Law

ChatGPT was a big deal. It was creepily relatable and everyone could access it, so we quickly worked ourselves into a frenzy. What does this witchcraft mean!? Companies cynically jumped on our frenzy and slapped "Now with AI!" all over their products, further whipping us up. But there's a great adage known as Amara's Law, after scientist and futurist Roy Amara, who coined it: We tend to overestimate the effect of a particular technology in the short run and underestimate the effect in the long run.

Let's look at communications: My grandmother was born in 1913 and lived to be over 100, passing away in 2014. She remembered her excitement at the first telephone installed in her house when she was a girl. But the Dick Tracy communication watch popularized by the comic book character when my grandmother was in her early twenties didn't arrive until the advent of the voice-enabled smartwatch when she was in her nineties. The gizmo still didn't gain widespread use until Apple released the third version of their smartwatch the year my grandmother passed away. On the other hand, in her last decade, she was an avid internet user, the impact of which she couldn't have envisioned when she made her first telephone call or read Dick Tracy comics. Impact overestimated in the near term (Dick Tracy watch), underestimated in the long term (internet).

Is Amara's Law true for AI? Are we overestimating in the short run (Terminator, killer robots) and underestimating in the long run (democratization of expertise, workforce disruption)? Economists describe production as the result of a combination of land (natural resources), labor, capital, and entrepreneurship. If you consider AI to be a form of automation (it certainly can be), then it will change the relationship between labor and other factors. Does that mean AI will put writers out of work? Yes and no. I'm glad I'm writing this book and not brief descriptions of menswear in an online catalog. Generation of that kind of text is a layup for modern AI. "The machine" has been taught by the digitized text written by generations of copywriters who came before. AI is already making it harder, likely soon impossible, to make a living as a writer of new descriptive catalog copy. In that sense, the answer is yes: AI will put some writers out of work. On the other hand, AI is helping me by improving autocorrect and providing helpful suggestions on brevity, arguably making it less intimidating to sit here and write my first book, so in that sense, the answer is no. For me. For now.

Let's take another look at how AI changes the relationship between labor and production. After a long day, I sometimes relax with a TV show called *How It's Made*. Each episode is a compendium of narrated video shorts documenting the making of things. Think hockey stick manufacturing, snack food production, and lumber milling. A narrator voices soothing descriptions of the "worker" and the "machine" acting in concert to mass produce wooden hockey sticks or stamp out cheese crackers from dough. Generally, the worker does less frequent tasks like dumping ingredients for cheese crackers into a giant mechanical mixer. The machine does the high-frequency, repetitive tasks like rolling dough, stamping out crackers, and packaging, while industrious instrumental music plays at a low volume in the background. In one memorable episode on milling dimensional lumber out of raw logs, the worker is a saw operator. The machine is a computer system that's been taught to look at the end of each log to determine the ideal cutting pattern to get the most valuable lumber with the least number of cuts. A camera feeds the machine an image of the end of the log. The machine calculates and projects a grid-like pattern of laser light on the end of the log to show the worker where to cut. The worker lines up the saw according to the machine-generated cut pattern, and the saw buzzes through the log. After each cut, the machine adjusts the laser light pattern to indicate the next cut. The worker flicks joysticks and taps pedals at high speed to move the log and the saw blade to match the laser-projected cut instructions of the machine. It is mesmerizing—a melding of worker and machine much more compelling than the spellchecker that saved me from spelling "laser" as "lazer."

In these cases, AI affects how land, labor, capital, and entrepreneurship combine to produce books and lumber. In both cases, labor for the most part loses out while capital and entrepreneurship win. This is the age-old story of increased productivity driven by automation. But consider the difference between the two anecdotes. The AI-enabled automation of cut planning or mechanical production is familiar. A previous, slower manual manufacturing step (lumber-cut planning) performed by expert sawyers was in part taken over by a faster machine, allowing one saw operator to process many more logs, almost certainly putting saw operators out of work. But the automation of intellectual skills like editing, copywriting, and revising for brevity? That's new.

Those jobs have never been under threat. The capability of modern AI to perform tasks that previously required human cognition threatens entirely new sectors of labor. We're going to delve deeply into this later on, but for now, consider these examples and Amara's Law as context for the rest of the book.

The Making Of Modern AI

ChatGPT blew up our feeds, birthed a black swan, and got you to the point that you picked up this book. But how did we get to ChatGPT in the first place? By traveling a long road leading to either a rocket-assisted jump into the shiny future or the edge of a cliff above raging rapids, depending on your point of view. (Joking. It's neither.) Wasn't artificial intelligence just an academic science experiment? For a long time, it seemed that way.

Artificial intelligence has been around and in the works since the 1950s. We're not going to delve into the details of the last seventy-five years of AI evolution here. We *will* look at AI through a theory of evolutionary biology called "punctuated equilibrium," where a species stays mostly the same for maybe ninety-nine percent of its time on Earth, then changes dramatically in a short period of time (Eldridge & Gould, 1972). Sound familiar? We're also going to look at the major jumps in evolution as changes in a silly but illustrative pretend recipe for AI.

Trust that we'll go into more detail in the next chapter, but for now, we're going to oversimplify the heck out of things. Artificial intelligence is made from three ingredients: data, computing power, and algorithms. Data is digital information such as web pages, banking transactions, and video from the camera in your new car. Computing power is the ability to perform math calculations on a computer chip. Algorithms are rules for performing math calculations.

Recipe for AI

100,000,000 cups of data

1,000,000 cups of computing power

1 tbsp of the best machine learning algorithm you can get

Separate data into two equal parts, setting one aside. Combine computing power and algorithm in a large bowl. Transfer to your stand mixer and add the first half of the data. Mix completely, then pour into a pan and bake in an electric oven. Check the AI repeatedly until it reaches an accuracy level equal to or better than a human. Remove to cool. Now, a really good recipe can be repeated. Repeat the whole process with the 50,000,000 cups of data you set aside, and go to the market for another million cups of computing power and another tablespoon of algorithm. Run through the recipe with the second half of the data. If you get the same result, congratulations!

The recipe for AI has always been the same—lots of data, lots of computing power, and a great algorithm. We could assemble lots of data. Smart people came up with new algorithms. But for most of the last seventy-five years, there wasn't nearly enough computing power to bake useful AI.

Research kicked off in the mid-1950s but stayed largely static for thirty years. This was our equilibrium. We needed 1,000,000 cups of computing power but only had two, so brilliant mathematicians and early computer scientists dreamed up beautiful algorithms partly inspired by the interconnected neurons of our brains, called "neural network" algorithms. In the 1980s, better computer hardware developed by among others, IBM, Sun Microsystems, and Thinking Machines Corporation finally caught up to these algorithms. This was the first jump in evolution, a punctuation of the equilibrium. The recipe still required 1,000,000 cups of computing power, which wasn't available, but we could still make a decent AI machine by fiddling with the algorithm and using the 10,000 cups of computing power in the computer we had. The AI of this era are sometimes known as expert systems. They were capable of performing highly specific tasks like calculating mortgage rates or monitoring the safety of hydroelectric dams. Think of a 1980's expert system as a healthy unleavened cake made with buckwheat and molasses. It's a cake, but not very good. Still, it was a major evolutionary jump—a big change in the equilibrium.

By the 2000s, neural network algorithms and the available computing power could be reliably used for specific tasks like handwriting recognition on bank checks. Given my own chicken-scratch handwriting, the fact that a computer could tell the difference between a 2 and a 7 on my checks was pretty cool. Another big jump in evolution.

Artificial intelligence research marched along for another fifteen years until the mid-2010s, when computer hardware again caught up with the newest "deep learning" algorithms. Deep learning algorithms are like stacks of multiple neural networks that mimic the multiple layers (deep) of interconnected neurons (neural network) in the human brain. We now had 100,000 cups of computing power in one computer, enough power to use a deep learning algorithm to teach a machine. The next step in evolution! Deep learning improved the ability of AI to deal with human language, enabling massive improvement in tasks like machine translation and voice recognition. Remember 2015, when many of us started saying, "Hey, Alexa," to oh-so-helpful (but sometimes creepy) devices we brought into our homes? They were surprisingly cheap for what they did but were always listening. We already know the next evolutionary leap happened around 2022. What sparked it this time?

Was it once again more computing power? Actually, no. Turns out that not long after 2015, we got to the required 1,000,000 cups of computing power in one computer. Was it more data? No, we had more of that than ever before. Ironically, for the first time, we had more of both ingredients than we could use! But we were still stuck because, even with all that computing power, it would still take decades for the deep neural network algorithms to process all the available data. This was because you had to do everything on one computer, a bottleneck that limited how much a machine could learn. The key ingredient was a fresh new algorithm that could be mixed with data and as much computing power on as many computers as you could throw at it. This new algorithm could be used to teach AI in weeks or months instead of years or decades.

In 2017, a group of researchers at Google published a research paper describing a new kind of deep learning algorithm called a "Transformer." The paper is titled "Attention Is All You Need" (Vaswani et al., 2017). In it, they show how the Transformer algorithm figures out how much attention to pay to relationships between words. For example, the Transformer can figure out that the relationship between "ice" and "cream" is worth paying attention to, while "ice" and "pizza" don't have anything to do with each other. That way when you ask it to complete the sentence, "I like to eat ice…" it'll give you "I like to eat ice cream." Prior to this approach, algorithms would "re-read" the same whole sentence over and over to figure out what a sentence meant. Relying on attention turned out to be a better way to teach a machine to "understand" complex language, and it turns out that it was a more efficient algorithm for a computer to run, too. This meant that in our recipe the Transformer needed only 900,000 cups instead of 1,000,000 cups of computing power. And it got better results on standard language translation tasks (English to German and English to French). Now we could use the Transformer algorithm in our AI recipe to bake the best AI ever and still have 100,000 cups of computing power left over. But the earth-shattering thing about the Transformer was that it could take one big job (understand a long paragraph) and divide it up into lots of little jobs (understand a word, phrase, or sentence). In the world of AI, that meant you could divide up the job of teaching a machine among hundreds of thousands of computers instead of just one. Computers that all talk to each other over super-fast network connections to arrive at the answer. This divide and conquer approach is called "parallel computing."

Ten percent less expensive (in computing power), with a better result on a longstanding benchmark *and* the ability to do things in parallel was a very big deal. The paper set off a race to develop the next AI among the big "tech" companies that many years before had actually become big "data" companies. For decades, Google/Alphabet, Facebook/Meta, Amazon, and Microsoft harvested every scrap of our (and our kids') data they could get away with. They invested their massive profits into mind-numbingly huge numbers of computers, which they made yet more money on by renting out as "cloud" computing. All hoped to one day, someday, maybe win the AI race. It's ironic that Google invented the algorithm but still lost the AI race, even though its hybrid corporate/academic "Brain" division hosted and funded the research that produced the Transformer algorithm. Google Brain had attracted leading researchers to work at Google with the promise of intellectual freedom (work on what you find interesting) and academic credit (publish your discoveries). These were scientists who chose to be professors at universities because they didn't want corporate bosses telling them what to work on, and who wanted to share the new knowledge they created with humanity. Brain attempted a win-win where researchers had freedom of inquiry and could share their discoveries while Google could support and benefit from their work. Google Brain researchers published the "Attention Is All You Need" paper in an open online journal and their code on an open-source website for anyone in the world to use—including engineers at a two-year-old startup called OpenAI.

OpenAI took the Transformer and ran with it, ultimately creating ChatGPT. They had billions to spend on data acquisition and cloud computing power from their investors, and they incorporated as a nonprofit, so they were able to attract the often mission-oriented best and brightest scientists and engineers. The good people at OpenAI scraped all the words on all the web pages ever published on the internet and engineered their own version of the Transformer: The Generative Pretrained Transformer, better known as GPT, which quickly led to ChatGPT and Sam Altman's decision to release ChatGPT in 2022 whether we were ready or not. In Chapter One, we'll return to how AI works, but now we'll tackle the most basic question: If AI is so great, why am I and everyone I know freaked out by it?

Agency Is What You Need

Artificial intelligence learns from the data we create in our digital lives, and artificial intelligence is taught by what we deem "intelligent" (or not) when interacting with just about every digital tool we use.

Today, you are teaching AI with every "like" button you click, every star rating you give, every purchase in one of the many AI-enabled convenience stores, every notification on your phone you respond to (or don't), every automated text message you reply to, every click on a search page, every drive you take with a navigation app, and on and on. If you feel like the digital world is constantly clamoring, vying, and demanding your attention, you're right. Artificial intelligence companies have adapted the Transformer algorithm to learn from your behavior, not just your words. Your likes, ratings, and views are used to teach Transformer-based AI what attracts attention. Attention is the new gold to be harvested from humans, now that we've handed over our data. Do you get sucked into social media? Do your parents? Your kids? Go easy on them and yourself. Social media companies spend billions of dollars on AI that knows what will grab your attention and when to show it to you so you spend more time in the app. It's almost like they learned from the cigarette companies, who figured out how to deliver nicotine so their product was more addictive. Oh, wait! Do an internet search for "meta addictive" and read more.

We are active participants in a system that completely depends on us while it also influences, changes, and sometimes manipulates our lives. Yet we have zero control, influence, or say in how AI is developed or injected into our world. It's as if Gutenberg built the first printing press by putting the twelve million people who read printed books to work in the shop helping him cast the moveable type. That's why we feel helpless. Why we feel resigned. Why we hunker down and hope for the best. That is when we're not afraid.

Because AI is scary. Multigenerational scary. Leaving aside apocalyptic science fiction, people of all ages see that, whether we like it or not, we're teaching machines that have the potential to do real and lasting harm. Just about every technological innovation from our past has been embraced by younger generations and feared by older generations. When it comes to AI, teens and twentysomethings, as well as the middle-aged, and the "most experienced" of us share unease at best. This book was inspired by a similarly titled lecture I started giving when I saw family, friends, people in my community, and professional colleagues wrestling with their fears. People of all generations came to these talks, which means that all generations care and are engaged. Young and "more experienced" alike shared anecdotes and asked variations on the same questions rooted in fear of the road ahead.

Survival Signals

Our fears and anxieties around AI may be broken down and grouped into what I call the "five D's" of Destruction, Deception, Dumbing Down, Disconnection, and Displacement.

Destruction is the fear of runaway AI causing us physical harm: killer robots, homicidal computers with disembodied voices, and autonomous cars running down pedestrians.

Deception is the fear of bad actors using AI to scam us: a fake voice or video of a trusted person in our lives used to steal, fake images used to cause embarrassment, and complex misinformation campaigns carried out automatically by AI.

Dumbing Down is the fear that our kids, our doctors, even we ourselves will take the easy way out with AI and we'll be worse off: AI does my homework (and I don't learn), AI makes the diagnosis (and perpetuates some bias).

Disconnection is the fear that AI will further reduce the real-life social interactions that make human life worth living.

Displacement is the fear that AI will make our work less valuable by automating some or all of it: AI writes my book better/faster/cheaper, AI analyzes financial data better than I can.

But here's the good news: Fear and our "gut" instinct are a big part of how we humans thrive as a species. Our gut instinct is actually a very real and powerful intuition that allows us to quickly see possible, even likely, outcomes without going through a more time-consuming stepwise logical analysis. When these outcomes might be bad, our subconscious intuition gives us what security specialist and author Gavin de Becker called the "gift" of the emotion fear. Fear, in turn, amplifies our intuition into an almost magical state of threat assessment. We are mostly conditioned by evolution to respond to physical threats, but as I contemplated my own fear of AI, I found an interesting parallel in the same signals we use to detect and avoid bodily harm.

In *The Gift of Fear* (1998), author Gavin de Becker helps us understand seven "survival signals" that can reveal a bad actor. Forced teaming, charm, too many details, typecasting, loan sharking, unsolicited promises, and discounting the word "no" are all tactics de Becker describes as the tools of manipulators, people who put their own interests above yours to your detriment. We can all use our intuition to watch out for these tactics and use them to spot people trying to manipulate us at the dawn of AI, in particular the companies and commercial interests almost exclusively driving AI in the U.S. at the time this book was being written. You'll notice that a lot of advertising and social media apps draw on these tactics to subconsciously influence our behavior.

Forced teaming is when AI or an AI company gets into our lives by *the projection of a shared purpose or experience where none exists.* Think about the advertisements you were seeing for AI at the time at the time of this book's publication. Google depicts AI as this happy helper on your phone that makes your photos better. Apple depicts AI as a reassuring, benevolent force in all its products that is there for you to make your life better in innumerable ways. Amazon's Alexa and "Hey Google" make the actors smile while they warmly weave AI into their happy home lives. The corporations behind these tools are singularly invested in your purchase of their products. They might not be evil, but they're not going to show up for you when you're broke and can't pay the subscription fee.

Charm is when an AI or AI company does everything it can *to compel, to control by allure or attraction.* Becker advises, *think of charm as a verb, not a trait. If you consciously tell yourself, 'this person is trying to charm me,' as opposed to 'this person is charming,' you'll be able to see around it.* The financial interests pushing AI on us do everything they can to *charm* us into using their products. In the cases where we are allowed to know AI is at work, interfaces pour out buckets of niceness. Alexa's voice and "her" choice of words are sweet and reassuring. ChatGPT is unfailingly polite when it is saddened that it cannot address our prompt. All the while, the AI and the business behind it are charming us into dependence to get us to part with our money.

Too many details is when AI or bad actors in the AI industry *cloud the context of what's actually happening by deliberately distracting or overwhelming us.* On the other hand, helpful context is when it's clear what AI is doing, how it's doing it, and what the effects are. De Becker writes that *context is always apparent at the start of an interaction...but too many details can make us lose sight of it.* When it first came out, ChatGPT had a pretty obvious context. It was presented as a research-grade tool, standalone, separate from your interactions with the rest of the digital world. It answered questions and wrote letters. The context was clear. A year later, everything around us was "powered by AI," with no meaningful explanation, only a fire hose of acronyms like LLM, GPT, and the word "generative" in every sentence. At the time of this writing, Google presented AI-powered search results at the top of their search page as authoritative with only a faint *generative AI is experimental* in a smaller, lighter font. *After* you clicked "show more" and *after* all the content. Click yet another very small and faint *learn more* and you were taken to a separate page with a lot of details and generalizations about how helpful AI may be but absolutely no real explanation of what it was doing, what "generative" meant or what the effect of using AI might be—distracting and overwhelming!

Typecasting is when an AI company's message *...involves a slight insult, and usually one that is easy to refute.* Look to the trend in advertising where we're made to feel "less than" if we don't invite the latest whiz-bang AI and technology into our lives. Apple's first advertisements for "Apple Intelligence" depicted people being dumb and lazy, until Apple Intelligence saved the office idiot by drafting a pithy email to his boss or made the forgetful husband look good by creating a last-minute heartwarming video for his wife's birthday. The unsubtle message is that you're a mouth-breathing dummy and need Apple Intelligence to save you from yourself. The German software company SAP ran advertisements in airports all over the world telling us, "You'll never have all the right answers. But your AI can." They're hoping you leap to your feet, thinking, "I can have the right answers! I'll tell my IT department to buy SAP AI!"

Loan sharking is when an AI company *generously offers assistance but is always calculating the debt.* The day I wrote this paragraph, you could buy Amazon's newest AI Echo Dot for delivery in Germany for €64 ($67). The same day, the same *hour*, you could buy the exact same device in the U.S. for $22! Germans are protected by modern comprehensive data use laws. Americans are not. Alexa is offering to assist Americans for one-third of the cost, but as we'll see later, you may be surprised by what she can do with your data.

The unsolicited promise is *used to convince us of an intention but with no guarantee.* Watch for when AI companies appear to solve your problem but do not in any way provide a guarantee. It's always a good idea to take a minute to figure out who is left holding the bag when things go wrong. For example, if you ask Google's AI a question about legal matters, its answer is presented at the top of the page in a way that looks visually authoritative. You are welcome to take the answer and run with it. But if you click "show more" and scroll to the fine print, you may see another subdued disclaimer. This time *Generative AI is experimental. For legal advice, consult a professional.* When you buy a car with an AI Advanced Driver-Assistance System, you may have responded to advertising showing a relaxed person traveling down the road with the promise that the car is taking care of everything. But that is not a guarantee! Every time you tap the warning message on the screen in the car at startup, you've signed a contract that you and your insurance policy guarantee the safety of the car. You hold the liability bag if the car's AI decides to follow faint lines on the road and swerve into the car next to you.

Discounting the word "no" is when the fine print governing just about every AI tool Americans use starts with the words, "By using the service you agree…" and somewhere in the middle includes "…to grant us an unrestrictive, free, worldwide license to your data.…" But if the choice is to use AI-driven Microsoft Word and give up control of your data or refuse and become irrelevant without the ability to use the world's main word processing program do you really have a choice? You may say “no,” but then what?

You’re right to be intuitively wary of AI because it’s being served to us with all of these tactics. It’s natural to be afraid. I am. But I try to use that fear to motivate myself to take charge, learn, and use AI to maximum benefit in my life and the lives of people I care about. I try to resist letting fear become paranoia or justification to barricade the door and simply hope for the best. Fear helps us realize there will be unintended consequences from AI. Fear also helps us motivate to put ourselves in a less vulnerable position.

While big corporations are doing what they’re legally required to do, maximize shareholder return, there’s nothing intrinsically bad about AI. It’s just a machine. It can even do amazing good. For example, one of the most important projects I worked on during my time at the Children’s Hospital of Philadelphia was figuring out how to use AI to scale up and share the expertise of the very, very few pediatric radiologists who can reliably differentiate a rib fracture sustained in a bike accident from a rib fracture resulting from child abuse. Physicians and researchers are teaching machines to make the distinction so children in towns without an expert radiologist can be protected. As scared of AI as I am, I can’t just throw it away because I know the good it is capable of.

If you realize how much agency you have as a consumer, parent, employee, and voter you can choose how AI does and doesn’t impact your life, how AI can be used for good. AI, by its very nature, must learn from *you*. Without you, AI has no way to learn what’s relevant, what's right or wrong, and therefore has no value. Your data and the context of your life are what make AI work. You teach the machines.

Our goal is to be drivers, not passengers. Be the windshield, not the bug. You create the data to teach AI. You teach AI the right answers, what's funny, if music is good, and how to do the most important tasks. This book will help you understand AI, warts and all. It will help you try out AI out, to see what it can do to make your life and work better and more valuable. Remember, it's up to you. *You* teach the machines!

Exercises: Try It Out

Throughout this book, I'll share some of the things I've done to learn about AI by using AI. Just as there were no experts when the Internet and the World Wide Web came to be in 1993, there are no experts in the use of AI. It's all new and changing fast. There is no "they" as in "they are smarter, more experienced at using AI." The field is divided only between the people who start to use AI and the people who don't.

This means that whether you have used AI or not, you are not behind. My goal with this book is to help you get comfortable with AI if you have not done so already. Some of these exercises may seem basic, others may challenge you to stretch. I encourage you to try them all.

Spell Check—example of pattern-recognition behavior that augments our spelling

--Use your phone to type a new text message, or use your computer to type a new document. Misspell "their" as "thier," and see what happens.

Autocomplete—example of "generative" behavior that augments our spelling and writing and helps us search things more quickly

--Do a web search using your phone or computer. Type in "what is" and look at the list of suggestions. These are generated from the first two words you typed in.

--Add autocomplete in email. It will finish your sentence for you based on what you've typed in the past or what it thinks you should say. It can be annoying sometimes!

Autofocus—example of a feedback and optimization behavior that augments our ability to quickly take good pictures

--Open the camera app on your phone. Sit at a table and put a drinking glass or other similar object on the table in front of you. Hold your phone so the glass is in the foreground of the screen. Tap on the image of the glass, then tap on the image of something farther away.

References

de Becker, Gavin, 1998. *The Gift of Fear: And Other Survival Signals That Protect Us from Violence*. Dell.

Eldridge, Niles, & Stephen Jay Gould, 1972. *Punctuated Equilibria: An Alternative to Phyletic Gradualism. Models in Paleobiology.* (Retrieved on April 28, 2025, from Punctuated equilibria: an alternative to phyletic gradualism // (1972) pp 82-115 in "Models in paleobiology", edited by Schopf, TJM Freeman, Cooper & Co, San Francisco. : Eldredge, N. & Gould, S.J. : Free Download, Borrow, and Streaming : Internet Archive)

Erasmus, Desiderius, 1515. *Sileni Alcibiadis.* Froben.

Erasmus, Desiderius, 1516. *The Education of a Christian Prince.* in [a]edibus Ascensianis.

Finkel, Irving, & Jonathan Taylor, 2015. *Cuneiform: Ancient Scripts*. J. Paul Getty Museum.

Houston, Keith, 2016. *The Book: A Cover-to-Cover Exploration of the Most Powerful Object of Our Time*. W. W. Norton & Company.

Kerr, James M, 1991. *The IRM Imperative: Strategies for Managing Information Resources*. Wiley.

Taleb, Nassim Nicholas, 2010. *The Black Swan: The Impact of the Highly Improbable*. (2nd ed.). Random House.

Vaswani, Ashish, Noam Shazeer, Niki Parmar, et al., 2017. *Attention Is All You Need.* ACM Digital Library. (Retrieved on May 8, 2025, from *Attention is All You Need* | Proceedings of the 31st International Conference on Neural Information Processing Systems)

CHAPTER 1:

What is AI?

You may never directly teach AI yourself, but as we discussed in the Introduction, you participate in the process just about every time you interact with the digital world. You may also be in an organization that is considering if and how to adopt AI tools. These days, it is highly likely that an eager executive will push to "do something with AI" in your organization. These words are music to the ears of vendors who spend big money marketing their products as "powered by AI" whether they are or not. You can add a lot of value by understanding how AI learns so you can ask hard questions and set realistic expectations in your life and for your organization. You can be a big part of the solution by understanding and helping to position potential AI tools in the context of specific problems and human work that's already happening. We'll get into this more in the next chapter but, for now, know that the few AI projects that succeed are the ones that focus hard on context and people up front. Successful AI projects answer the question, "Just because we can, should we?"

"Daddy! I can't get the !@#$% sand out of my shoes!" The tiny voice from the back seat of the car was my three-year-old daughter appropriately vocalizing profanity for the very first time. I was simultaneously horrified, proud, curious, and (let's be honest) amused. Her still-developing intelligence had for the first time understood the perfect context for profanity and nailed it. My wife and I had not specifically taught her to swear when she wasn't able to shake sand out of her little sneakers. She had (unfortunately) heard my wife and me swearing in other situations, none of which involved sand or shoes. She had gathered information from those specific cases and correctly applied it to an entirely new situation with which she had no prior experience.

When we encounter AI that can do something similar, we see intelligence in the machine. We marveled at the unveiling of ChatGPT because the underlying AI could take completely off-the-wall input it had never seen before and come back with a reasonable response in the appropriate context. My daughter had never been strapped into her car seat with a shoe full of unwanted sand, but her developing brain had been exposed to enough unrelated situations to figure out that this was a four-letter-word moment. This is what psychologists call "transduction," a form of reasoning where developing children learn from specific cases they experience and apply their new knowledge to general (new) cases they haven't experienced. Much of machine learning and AI, including the Transformer developed by Google, are conceived to solve general transduction problems, along with a related type of problem called "sequence modeling," discussed in the next paragraph. The Transformer, invented by researchers at Google in 2017 and developed into AI applications in many languages, could similarly encounter an English sentence it had never seen before—such as,

"What do I say in German when I am very frustrated because I can't get the sand out of my shoe?"—and come up with "Ich bekomme den @#$% sand nicht aus meinem schuh!"

Here's another example of the human brain at work. Consider this series of words: *pine*, *sauce*, *crab*. What's the next word in the series? If you quickly guess "pie," "Adam's," or "computer," you are using your instinctive powers of reasoning to subconsciously assess the relationship between the first three words and find something they have in common—in this case "apple"—to inform your choice of the next word. You can also puzzle this out through a more deliberate process of elimination using your analytical brain. This may be slower, but it can also lead to the correct answer more often. We're all wired for both instinctual insight and analytical thinking, though individually we often skew one way or the other (Kounios & Beeman, 2015). Your brain is built for instinctual insight, so the more language you're exposed to, the more likely it is that your brain quickly finds a relationship between the first three words in the sequence to use as context to come up with a fourth word. This type of cognition is part of something called "fluency," where pathways in your brain have been trained by repeated exposure to information. Your fluent pathways are strengthened when you subconsciously create a common associate like "apple" between remote associates like "pine," "sauce," and "crab," all words or concepts that don't share an obvious connection. When you make up a mnemonic, such as a silly limerick, to help you remember something, you're using the same underlying cognitive mechanism. We see intelligence when we encounter machines that can mimic sequential insight like this in a general way. Picking what comes next is the type of problem in both psychology and machine learning called "sequence modeling." These are very important problems for humans. Figuring out what happens next, or even the few possibilities that *might* happen next, is a big part of how we are successful as a species. We are especially impressed when the answer isn't something we would have come up with on our own. Just as in the example with my daughter, the key to intelligence is that the machine, the AI, performs well when it comes across something it hasn't ever encountered before. That general capability sets AI apart from other kinds of computer programs that work under tighter constraints.

Does this mean everything called AI around us is able to solve general problems? Nope. Software companies desperately want to take advantage of the excitement over AI by slapping the AI label on their products. But a computer system is not AI just because it follows rules to do useful work, no matter how slick the packaging. Rules are created by looking at a bunch of specific cases, then writing up the logic for what to do in those cases. Think back to the semi-automated sawmill example in the Introduction. That computer system was likely programmed based on an old, expert-authored manual of rules for how to saw a log into valuable lumber. What magic there is comes from the clever detection of the outline of the log in a digital photograph, which is itself based on geometric and mathematical rules for finding the edge of a simple, predictable shape. This is by far the best and most efficient way to solve that particular problem. It would be a waste of time and money to show an AI a bunch of logs and a bunch of lumber and teach it to come up with the right cut pattern. One goal of this book is for you to be able to ask questions and think critically about what does and doesn't deserve to be called AI, and even more important, to assess which kinds of problems are worth the effort and uncertainty that come with AI. Because teaching a machine takes a lot of work, and you usually don't know what you're going to get.

How Machines Learn

How do machines learn? Scientists work hard to use the human brain as a model for learning intelligence. After all, they don't have much else to go on! The starting point for *artificial* intelligence is informed—at least at a high level—by our understanding of the design of the brain and theories of how we learn.

Your brain is a giant mass of interconnected cells called neurons. But it's more than just a skull full of neuron spaghetti. Neurons are elongated cells that form the wiring of your brain. Each neuron cell listens for a signal from nearby neurons. When the signal gets strong enough, the cell activates and sends its own signal out to its neighboring neurons, propagating patterns of signals through the different parts of your brain. Take, for example, your eyes looking at a brightly lit square of paper, half white, half black. Nerve endings in your eye are excited by nearby light-sensitive cells that pop off a signal. That signal tells your neurons to transmit their own signal, but in a pattern that reflects the pattern of light and dark hitting the back of your eye. The pattern of signals travels down what is effectively a data cable from your eye to your brain.

The signals dump into your brain where the arrangement of neurons isn't just random, but is organized into neighborhoods, or specialized networks, where the neurons in the network are particularly good at specific kinds of signaling. For example, detecting a bright light. These networks are organized into layers that are good at specific kinds of thinking. You can think of the layers as a stack of pancakes, where the top pancake of networked neurons does the simplest task like measuring overall brightness at different grid coordinates. That layer hands the map of what's bright and what's not to the next layer, which detects edges in the image—the outline of the square and the boundary between the black and white sides. Your brain continues this general organization where each layer takes input, uses its network of neurons to process it to some degree, then hands off the result to the next layer (Gazzaniga, 2018). For example, when you look at your dog, your eyes send a bunch of electrical signals representing brightness, contrast, and color to the layer of your brain that is your visual cortex. Your visual cortex takes that input and turns it into signals that it hands off to other layers of the brain that do a specific job. There are layers to store and recall memories ("That's my dog, Lilo"), set off emotions ("I love my big baby girl, Lilo"), create speech ("Come here, big baby"), and move our hands (scratch, scratch, scratch). We've been trained by our repeated experiences of the world around us to recognize, feel love for, interact with, and pet our dog. As we grow and develop as children, we learn to recognize all sorts of animals, like kangaroos and deer, but unless we're living in a zoo, we don't moon over them and scratch their ears. But we can tell them apart from dogs!

Similarly, AI systems are designed to use pretend digital equivalents of neurons, networks, and layers to process information. So far, we've talked about language AI, but there is a whole world of visual AI as well. Take a learning task like figuring out if a picture contains (a) a dog or (b) no dog. A visual AI has a layer that takes in a collection of numbers representing the intensity, color, and position of all the dots (pixels) that together make up a digital photo. That input layer hands the raw data off to the next layer, which figures out what's bright and what's dark, then hands everything off to the next layer which figures out where there is something that humans would recognize as an edge, or line. The next layer figures out which lines are organized into simple shapes. The next layer determines which shapes are important and hands those off to the final layer, which makes a guess as to whether one of the shapes is a dog. Just as in our brains, each layer in the AI doesn't care what the other layers do; it's good at its one task. And just like in our brains, when you put all the layers together, you may get intelligence. Remember "deep learning" from the Introduction? Before 2015, machine learning was done with a single, flat neural network. "Deep" just means you have more than two layers besides the input and output layer. There's no magic number of layers in an AI "brain." You decide how many layers to start with, based on the type of AI and the kind of learning. When you teach a machine from scratch, the only layer you specifically set up is the first input layer.

The layers after that aren't set up ahead of time to do anything specific. They all start out as generic collections of digital neurons. A new AI has to *learn* what to do layer by layer. All this adds up to what gets loosely called an "algorithm."

Layers are as far as we're going to go in terms of AI's internal wiring. There are many wonderful books you can read to delve into the fascinating and beautiful construction of AI algorithms. Or you can ask your favorite AI to explain it to you, though I'd recommend a combination. But for practical purposes, the algorithm is just the starting point. The magic happens when you teach the algorithm to do something truly remarkable.

The General Systems Theory of psychology attempts to explain human behavior by looking at the three main variables of human psychology: biological (hungry), psychological (decide to seek food), and social/behavioral (somebody feed me). If you're a baby, you get the inputs your body needs (food) by controlling your outputs (crying in a tone that means hungry vs uncomfortable from a wet diaper). You output information (crying) to your environment by planning actions to get what you want. In a system, this is called "feed-forward." The actions you plan (time to cry) are based on a guess of the consequences of those actions (Dad feeds me). You run the plan (cry) and compare the actual consequences with what you thought they'd be (did I get fed or not?). This is called feedback. If you didn't get what you wanted (still hungry), you adjust the plan (cry louder), which is using feedback (McConnell, 1989). The teaching of machines, machine learning, is all about infant computer programs going through the cycle of planning actions and guessing consequences (feed-forward), doing the actions, then comparing the actual result to the guessed result (feedback), adjusting if necessary to repeat the cycle (using feedback).

We're going to dig into an example of how AI is taught by people and deployed into the real world. Before we get there, it's helpful to understand the general approach to machine learning along with some of the technical terms for key parts of the process and steps that are applied.

First, you need a topic or situation based in the real world. Artificial intelligence, like humans, needs to focus on one thing at a time while learning, so in our AI, we focus on a specific topic to provide loose boundaries. We call this topic the domain. The Google Brain team chose foreign languages as the domain when they were developing and testing their Transformer. In our example, the domain is "dogs." Within the general topic, we go further and articulate a particular problem to solve. This problem is called the task. Our task is "Decide if a picture has a dog in it, or not." Next is a definition of success. I can't overstate how critical it is to decide on and define the successful outcome we want ahead of time. Your measure of success is called the metric. Recall that Google's Transformer was first taught to pass a longstanding standardized test of English-to-German and English-to-French language translation. This was their metric, or measure of success. With AI, you're teaching a machine to approximate or augment a cognitive process that only a human can do, so you or your organization MUST understand baseline human performance and articulate ahead of time what success looks like for the AI. Your measure of success is called the metric. The AI doesn't have to "beat the human" like the chess-playing computers from the 1990s. It's enough to set a standard that the AI helps a human to accomplish faster. Our example metric is "Find more than 90% of the dog pictures." This metric is the critical educational outcome that guides how you teach the machine. The next step is to procure the equivalent of a textbook for AI training: enough relevant data for the lesson. How much data is enough? Enormous, truly huge volumes of data are required to successfully teach AI. You need to start with every scrap of data relevant to your problem that you can beg, borrow, or steal (not really). It will likely still not be "enough." This is why the most successful AI research, and the most successful AI products, come from huge companies that spend billions and decades collecting our data. We call this the training data.

Our example data set is six thousand family photos, some with the dog, some without. Your AI will study the data you give it, reading or looking at it over and over. The sum of what it learns during this process depends on the volume and quality of data you provide. The data has to be described and characterized by humans so you know the answers ahead of time, just like an instructor's answer key in a textbook. We call this labeling. For our example, three different veterinarians each looked at all six thousand pictures and labeled each "dog" or "no dog." The final step in preparing to teach is the design of the empty, untrained brain of the AI. What kind of brain? How many layers? How do the layers talk with each other? This is called the model architecture. We choose Residual Network, since it's a well-tested architecture for image recognition. You can treat it as a black box, so we won't go into more detail.

Now you teach! You organize a repeated series of lessons and quizzes where the AI does the feed-forward part of learning. It uses its untrained brain to look at a randomly selected set of *half* of the dog pictures. This half of the total data set is called the training data. The AI does the task of predicting the right answer (dog or no dog) and then takes a quiz where you check its prediction against the human labels. After each quiz, you use a computer program to give the AI feedback on what it got right and wrong. It uses the feedback to adjust how its brain re-reads the data and comes up with answers (a mathematical process called gradient descent). You repeat for potentially hundreds of cycles of training so the different layers in the AI brain learn to do specific tasks, much as the layers in a baby's brain learn their job in the larger task of recognizing animals or getting someone to feed them. During the repeated cycles of training, the AI develops an equivalent to fluency from repetition and by learning hidden gems like how a common associate such as the combination of dark nose and round eye shape ties together remote associates like German shepherd, pug, and beagle. You stop the cycle of lessons and quizzes when the AI gets a good score a few times in a row, better than ninety percent correct on our metric, and it's clear it isn't learning anymore. This repeated good score is called convergence. If you want to impress someone when they are bragging about their AI, ask them, "How many training cycles before convergence?"

Now for the final exam. The AI reads the other half of data it's never seen before, called the testing data set, and does the task just once for this other half of the data, called the testing data set. Remember, the data is labeled by experts, so you know the answers to the test. If the AI passes the test and hits your predetermined metric of correctly identifying ninety percent of the dog pictures, it gets a good grade, and you celebrate! This final exam is the proof that AI can learn enough from a specific case where it has access to the answers (training) and then successfully generalize to a case it's never seen before where you know the answer but it does not (testing).

Much like a new graduate, your AI now has theoretical knowledge but hasn't been out in the real world where it really counts. The really hard part of this process is launching your newly trained AI out into the real world (deployed), but in a way that allows it to continue learning safely. The task may be low stakes like identifying pictures of dogs and relatively easy to deploy or high stakes like pointing out bone fractures on x-rays and relatively hard to deploy. No matter, training is just the first step before figuring out how to get your AI from the classroom into the real world (deployed). You'd think after all that, you'd be done. Unfortunately, newly graduated AI is destined to fail unless it is deployed in a way that allows it to continue learning on the job because it is simply impossible for your training to include every possible scenario, or combination of data. Remember, the whole *point* of AI is that it can do good work when it encounters things it's never seen before. Much like a well-educated person, AI that keeps learning on the job can use its training, and now experience, to solve problems in a changing environment (continual learning).

Now we'll use a real example to review the terms domain, task, metric, data, labeling, training, gradient descent, convergence, testing, deploying, and continual learning

I recently visited Iceland for the first time. On our way through the glacial areas of the Southwest we went on a hike from a barren, regularly flooded volcanic plain into an older, sheltered valley with plenty of trees. Songbirds suddenly appeared and chirped their hearts out as soon as we got into trees that were more than waist high. Iceland has plenty of trees, but they rarely grow more than five or six feet tall due to the heavy wind and wild swings in the amount of daylight, from twenty-four hours of light in the summer to twenty four-hours of dark in the winter. The rapid appearance of birds made me aware of the absence of birdsong everywhere else in Iceland, something I take for granted as background noise living in the U.S. mid-Atlantic region. So I got curious about birdsong and remembered hearing about an AI-powered birdwatching app called Merlin. Merlin is the result of a wonderful citizen-scientist collaboration at Cornell University. The coolest part of the app is an AI feature called "Sound ID" that can identify more than four hundred and fifty bird species in the U.S. and Canada alone from brief recordings you make of the world around you. The goal of the Merlin team was to capture the knowledge and expertise of a relatively few expert birdwatchers and share it with as many people as possible so they may also learn how to identify the birds around them. Think back to our historical precedents for AI: the invention of writing by the ancient Sumerians and the invention of the modern printing press by Johannes Gutenberg. Before writing and printing, a birdwatcher, or more likely a bird hunter, could teach at most a few other people to track birds by verbally describing what to listen for: "If you hear a repeated metallic chirp followed by a sort of up-and-down trilling, it's a bunting." Writing, then printing, and by extension, the internet captured that knowledge so that many more could benefit, and a few centuries later, aspiring birdwatchers could listen to audio recordings, and then go stand in the backyard and try to pick out individual birds from the cacophony of birdsong around them. Now, AI in the form of Merlin puts the expertise of some of the most accomplished bird experts in the world in your pocket. It walks you through each call you're hearing and helps you learn what bird it belongs to. Merlin is used by hundreds of thousands of people, many of whom, despite the birdwatching books on their shelves, were unlikely to learn to identify birds without it. So let's take a look at how Merlin came to be.

Birds, like humans, are lifelong vocal learners (as are dolphins and bats). As chicks, they learn from their parents to both vocalize and understand sounds and they keep learning for the rest of their lives. Researchers discovered that birds use a form of cognitive language—their equivalent to words, grammar, and phrases—as more than communications signals. Birds will adjust and respond to changes in the order of chirps and warbles, which we anthropomorphize as grammar. In their own unique way, they will respond to minute changes in very high frequency parts of birdsong (Fishbein et al., 2019). Ornithologists, immersed in the study of birdsongs and bird language curated and labeled sound recordings and made them available to the public on the internet. Artificial intelligence researchers love freely available data that has already been characterized or labeled by experts because they can use it to train AI. Even more, AI researchers love *language* data in any form because its intricacies help to drive new discoveries, often relevant to cognition—the goal of AI. So AI researchers at the University of California San Diego doing early work with pictures of birds from the internet were thrilled when ornithologists at Cornell contacted them and invited them to check out the huge and growing collection of birdsong recordings at Cornell's Macaulay Library—at the time of this writing, more than 1,300 species (Galchen, 2024).

The scientists worked together to choose a *domain*—the topic for the AI—which in this case was bird vocalizations. The *task* for the AI—the particular problem it needed to solve—was identifying the bird that made a particular sound. The *metric*, or how they'd know if they got it right, was precision—how often the AI thought it was right *and it actually was*. The *data* were the one million recordings of birds in the Macaulay Library, many contributed by amateur bird watchers for research like this. They also included recordings of sounds you might hear together with birdsong out in the world, like wind, cars honking, and dogs barking. The *labels*—the answer key—were details *added* to each bird recording by citizen scientists (amateur birdwatchers) and expert ornithologists. The labeled data were divided into two halves, with the first half dedicated to training and the second to testing. The researchers chose a deep learning model architecture for the untrained brain called a residual network, a model architecture known for its flexibility.

The AI was trained by being made to "listen" to each type of bird to classify its species hundreds and hundreds of times, sometimes with background noises thrown in. The Merlin AI doesn't actually "listen" to anything. Much of the information contained in an audio recording of a bird singing (the level or volume of sound at different frequencies over a period of time) can also be represented in visual form as something called a spectrogram, and this is what the AI learned to recognize. You see spectrograms in movies and on TV when producers want to show you "sound waves." Children of the 1960s saw a crude spectrogram on *Lost In Space* when The Robot spoke, kids of the 1980s saw KITT's red fluctuating speech lights on the dashboard in *Knight Rider*, and millennials watching *Futurama* saw Bender the robot's crass speech mirrored in the wiggly lines of his mouth. So Merlin represents sound as a spectrogram image when it learns.

Each training cycle was followed by a quiz to see if the AI correctly identified the bird from its song. After each quiz, the AI was given feedback on how well it did. As it was trained, the AI used something called a "gradient descent calculation" to adjust the layers of its brain to optimize its learning. "Gradient" means the direction to adjust a layer to reduce errors. "Descent" means how much to adjust a layer. The AI went through cycles of training until it converged on a final level of performance (meaning it had learned all it could and wasn't getting any better). The trained AI was then tested with the other half of the labeled data it had not seen before to measure its precision (the final exam). Good news for budding amateur birdwatchers: it passed! The Merlin AI fits our definition of AI because it is a computer system taught by humans to do something no single human is likely capable of—recognize the unique song of thousands of birds worldwide.

The Merlin AI team then worked with app developers to deploy the AI into the Merlin app and set up the Merlin AI to continue to collect data and adjust its performance—what we call "continual learning"—based on the feedback of its users. If you use Merlin and give it feedback, then you teach the (Merlin) machine!

A Word About Data

We tend to trust knowledge and expertise when we have a sense that nobody's hiding anything. Our human educational system is built on a trusted combination of transparency, credentialling, and standardized evaluation. When someone is a trained, credentialed middle school science teacher, we generally know what to expect within a real-life range of ability. When a university professor teaches statistics or history to graduate students, the curriculum is overseen by a standards committee, the syllabus is almost always public, and the textbook or reading material is broadly published and available. You'll note that both the Merlin Sound ID AI and Google Brain's Transformer were trained using publicly available, well understood data. Both went on to have an impact on our world. That's not a coincidence. The best performing and most impactful AI will always come from transparent information. Would you accept a human teacher in your kids' school who used secret-sauce teaching materials that only they knew? Would you hire an expert who graduated from a university that used its own confidential "proprietary" textbooks and refused to be accredited by a third party?

AI is good and getting better at capturing human knowledge and approximating cognition, or thinking. It's good at breaking down bottlenecks and barriers to the use of expert knowledge by more people. It's also only as capable as we make it, since it's derived from the data in our world and the standard of "capable" set directly by us or indirectly by participating in digital systems where our judgment is captured. We trust AI when we trust the data it learned from, and we trust AI is "right" based on our own judgment or the impartial judgment of experts we trust. But this trust is not a given. A big part of teaching AI is selecting good data, finding ways to identify and ignore bad data, and then representing the data in a way that preserves the information we care about. There are whole fields of study and professions focused on these topics. If you're curious, look up "ground truth data" and "representation learning" to learn more.

The Language Of AI: Demystifying Jargon

As we begin incorporating AI into our lives, it's important to understand key terminology and to recognize the perils of advertising and marketing, gaslighting, and hype. For example, ChatGPT is AI, but not all AI is ChatGPT, as much as OpenAI would love for you to believe this. What follows is a glossary of AI terms that get thrown around a lot, some of which you have already encountered in this book. I provide a common sense, nontechnical explanation for each, and I encourage you to look up the terms that seem most important to you elsewhere—both for more detailed information and to understand how these technical concepts relate to each other. In fact, I strongly encourage you to learn as much about AI as you possibly can. You teach the machines.

But first a few words of advice. When you do a web search for some AI jargon, put the word "intuition" at the end. When I was in graduate school for computer science, I learned to ask professors to help me understand the intuition behind complex mathematical and computational concepts. This gave them room to separate hard facts and mathematical truth from the "gist," the overarching, big picture, human-relatable concept.

As much as possible, start with well-referenced or primary sources before turning to AI, if you use AI at all. For scientific and mathematical explanations, I often start with Wikipedia, as it's been hand-curated by people and experts over many years to be an accurate and useable reference. Please donate to Wikipedia at donate.wikimedia.org because the non-profit organization behind this website works tirelessly to empower hundreds of thousands of citizen experts to curate and fact-check knowledge. In return, all this freely given expertise is scraped off the Wikipedia website and used to train proprietary AI by the biggest, most profitable companies in the world. For those concerned with possible bias in Wikipedia articles, the organization offers an essay, "Wikipedia: Guide to Addressing Bias." However, Wikipedia cautions that the essay itself should be read with healthy skepticism.

Reddit is another helpful source because it captures the interaction and reasoning of its human contributors, with an up- or down-vote that can promote accurate information and demote baloney. But be brave and try to read primary scientific papers even if you don't understand most of what's presented. Another thing I've learned is that you can pick up important points from computer science, math, and other scientific papers without understanding all the details. You may be surprised. Plenty of "experts" don't understand what's in a paper the first time they read it. You can also learn about the progress of AI over time by seeing what papers are "highly cited" or referenced by other papers.

The point of further reading is to develop a sense of the field of AI. Know what you don't know. You may never become an expert, but this kind of reading can help you develop an intuitive sense of what is real vs hype, "magic" vs sleight of hand, distraction vs threat. Given the stakes and what's to come for our society and economy, a good bullshit detector is priceless.

I hope the definitions that follow are a helpful start at cutting through often overwhelming jargon and powering up your BS detector. Some of these terms and concepts appear earlier in the book, but since many of these topics are fairly abstract and complex, reading a more detailed explanation, along with additional examples, can be helpful. This is by no means a complete glossary, and the explanations are my own, based on study, work, and research in the field. They are intended to be conceptually and intuitively helpful, not thorough technical documentation. Please use this brief glossary as a starting point, and build on what's here by doing your own further reading and research.

The definitions, rather than appearing in alphabetical order, are organized in such a way that the terms logically follow one another.

Definitions

Algorithm—At the time this book was written, "algorithm" was used as a euphemism for artificial intelligence that seems to know something about us or the physical world. We use "algorithm" instead of artificial intelligence because it's a comfortable word to describe something that can get, well, creepy. Have you ever said or heard a friend say something like, "The algorithm knew I was thinking about buying a house!" followed by an uncomfortable laugh? But anytime you refer to the algorithms on Amazon or Instagram, you are in fact referring to AI.

The real definition of "algorithm" is a series of *readily explainable* mathematical instructions or formulas used to solve a problem. The equations and formulas of geometry are examples of actual algorithms. The circumference of a circle is two times its radius multiplied by the constant value of pi. $C = 2\pi r$. When it comes to AI, social media started with simple algorithms, initially based on your social network—people you connected with on the app. A lot has changed since then. In Meta's own words, "We began with manual feature engineering for small models and progressed to building hundreds of deep neural network models with trillions of parameters" (Meta, 2023). What exists now is possibly the most powerful, nonexplainable artificial intelligence directed at understanding and changing human behavior outside classified government surveillance. I refer to the artificial intelligence in social media as "my algorithm" when it shows me a video of a puppy, an advertisement for a powerful flashlight, and a political message that evokes an emotional response.

Social media companies are likely happy we call their AI systems "algorithms" because it's a less threatening and more marketable word. In the world of social media, artificial intelligence continually learns how to "engage" you, your parents, and your kids. "Engage" is a euphemism for "attract and hold your attention." The business model of every social media company is to "monetize engagement"—in other words, sell two things: advertisements and data about you. Your "algorithm" in reality is a personal artificial intelligence that knows how to hook you and keep you using social media for as long as possible. It continually learns what will attract your attention from behavioral data it collects directly, and also that it is receiving from every other app, website, navigation system, payment service, and physical business you give your email, phone number, or tracking cookie. You teach your own social media machine. And all this happens without the social media company really understanding *how* their artificial intelligence hooks you. They only care that it *does*. In my own life, what social media companies call engagement, I experience as addiction. I can't open up Instagram without getting sucked in. Before I know it, my "screen time" is up over four hours per day, a level of exposure researchers have found linked to increased symptoms of anxiety and depression (Zablotsky et al., 2024). Using "algorithm" to describe my social media AI is like using "vape" to describe a highly optimized electronic nicotine delivery device wrapped in child-friendly, colorful packaging, sold by companies that don't care *how* nicotine interacts with our brain to reinforce dependence, only that it does. End rant.

Data—When we're talking about AI, data are digital representations of the real or online world. Data are (or is; often data is treated as a collective noun) always a representative example of the real world, but almost never every possible representation. Since artificial intelligence learns by example, the more data you can give it, the more it can learn. Data can be *structured*, like a spreadsheet made up of columns and rows with numbers or text in each little box. Data can also be *unstructured*, like a digital photo, the electronic files used to hold the words of this book, or the squiggly line of your heartbeat on a monitor in the hospital. Humans can work with unstructured data as is; we can look at a picture and understand what we see or read this paragraph. Artificial intelligence, however, needs help. For the purposes of teaching artificial intelligence, all *unstructured* data must become structured. For example, the picture you took of a spring daffodil is transformed by a computer program into two columns of numbers with one row for every tiny little part of the picture. The bright area of white in the middle of the picture will produce many rows that give the coordinates of tiny little spots called pixels that make up the area. Each row will contain numbers representing the color and intensity at the exact spot. AI reads the structured data and learns from it. A 4K camera takes pictures that have 4000 rows!

"Wait, didn't you say there was AI in my car? But my car doesn't have eyes. How does it collect and use data?" Automotive AI, and just about every AI system that can respond to the physical world in real time (robots), uses sensors like cameras and accelerometers, along with computers on board that convert the images and brake force readings from unstructured to structured data that is then handed off to the AI. Automotive AI is initially taught using recordings made during millions of hours of cars driving around. That's part of what Google and others are doing when they send specially equipped camera cars to drive through your neighborhood. True story: It's gone now, but an early capture of my house by a Google Street View camera car showed my brother-in-law crouched between two parked cars acting like a monster about to pounce. He saw the camera car coming and hid between the cars. My brother-in-law created something called "noise" or an "outlier" in the data collected by Google, assuming he was the only random person pretending to be a monster that day. In addition to 360-degree cameras, these cars may also be equipped with radar and other sensors that capture distances, physical shapes, and motion, which can then be combined with the pictures to teach AI about the driving environment of our neighborhood.

Model—Collection of observations created by a computer system as it learns something from data. The following example is intuitive and easy to follow but completely made up and not actually true. If you're a pediatrician, please forgive me! Let's pretend I collect structured data from a thousand children by recording their weight at each birthday up to age fifteen. I make a spreadsheet with two columns, one for age, one for weight. I put my own data into the spreadsheet: At one year old, I was 10 pounds. At two years old, 22 pounds. Fifteen years old, 149 pounds. Let's pretend that same trend holds for most of the other children in the data. I can use a computer running a math equation (called linear regression) to learn a simple model, again not real but for illustration only:

The weight of a child is equal to ten times their age, plus or minus a few pounds.

The observations that make up the model are (a) that age is important to weight, (b) ten is the multiple that'll give you weight from age, and (c) we can expect a few pounds of error. Artificial intelligence models are learned from much more complex data (e.g., all the text ever published online) and contain many more observations, called "parameters"—sometimes into the tens of millions or billions—but a similar principle still holds. However, with both our fictional weight model and with artificial intelligence models, you have to remember that the model is only as useful as what it has "seen" before. The model learns parameters (observations) by example from the data it was given. To complicate matters further, AI parameters are never something understandable like "age." It's hard to think about, but the parameters (observations) in an artificial intelligence model are completely… artificial.

Because of the complexity involved, an AI model is not explainable in human terms; we treat it as a black box, a system where the precise internal workings are not known.

Foundation Model—A special kind of model used to represent a very broad area of our world or life. It could be as general and foundational as "the English language" or "pictures." Some of the first foundation models were indeed built from images. For example, a foundation model for images is a powerful tool to help artificial intelligence understand what makes up a line, basic shapes like squares and circles, light versus dark, and color. You can think of a foundation model as the part of your brain that processes the primary input from your eyes, ears, and other senses. You likely first experienced the power of a foundation model when your phone could unlock itself by looking at your face, then when you searched for a picture in the photo album on your phone. Foundation models based on language are the basis, in fact the *foundation,* of the powerful AI tools we started to use in the early 2020s. The next generation of foundation models is being built by the largest AI companies from multiple broad areas, for example, combining images and language.

Large Language Model—Foundation model built from human language. The machine has been taught the vocabulary, sentence structure, and style of an entire language. Additionally, the machine has been taught the likelihood of how words, sentences, and style occur together across an entire human language.

Machine Learning—The process of using a computer system to learn a model from data. Another (made-up) example: You need to forecast the global fish supply but have not been able to use regular math to figure out how water temperature, tide, location, and day of the year come together to determine how many fish will be caught. Your data contain the pounds of fish caught, water temperature, and height of the ocean tide at every minute of the day for a whole year at a thousand locations around the world. You decide to try machine learning: to teach a machine to guess whether fishing will be good.

Before you get started, you decide that if the machine can guess right more than three out of four times, it's a success. Then you train. You randomly select half of your data, give it to the machine, but hold back the answer of whether the fishing was good at each location. The machine guesses if the fishing was good, you tell it whether it got it right or wrong. It changes how it guesses and the cycle repeats. As it does a better job of guessing if the fish are biting, it creates its own secret parameters (observations) of what makes for good fishing. Eventually, it doesn't get any better at guessing and you record the parameters as your new fishing model. You've completed the training part of machine learning. Now you test the trained model by giving it the other half of the tide, time, and location data it's never seen before. Again, you know the right answer to whether the fishing is good. If the model (machine) guesses right at least three times out of four, you've successfully taught the machine. You've completed the testing part of machine learning. Importantly, somewhere in the layers of its neural network, the machine learned something you couldn't from all that data, some hidden factors nestled behind the data you do have. You'll never know what those factors are, but your new black box model does a pretty good job of guessing. Now you can use it to build a fish forecasting system that takes in water temperature, tide level, date, time, and location and tells a fisherman whether it's worth it to go out.

Artificial Intelligence—Computer systems that learn models from data through the process of machine learning. These models can "understand" (describe and represent) something like language, pictures of animals, x-rays, or rainfall. These models can also do tasks like translate languages, identify cats in pictures, diagnose broken bones, or predict rainwater runoff patterns.

Supervised—When a human tells a machine whether it guessed right or wrong. The fishing example above is supervised machine learning, supervised artificial intelligence.

Unsupervised—When a machine learns something that may or may not be "right" in the eyes of a human. On its own, without supervision. An example of unsupervised machine learning, or unsupervised artificial intelligence, would be when a machine learns which words are important on the Wikipedia website based on something like how often a word shows up in all the articles. You didn't teach it. Without supervision, it'll probably learn "and" is an important word. Unsupervised machine learning is often a first step in developing AI systems. After a round of unsupervised learning to get a rough model, humans can supervise the next round, during which you'll teach the machine to ignore "and," "the," and "is" in favor of words that you deem actually important.

Training—The part of machine learning when you tell a machine what it got right and wrong through multiple rounds of guessing. You know the answer (fishing is good or not), and the machine learns how to guess the answer based on the data you give it.

Testing—The part of machine learning where you show a freshly trained machine data it's never seen before and test whether it meets some benchmark you decided ahead of time.

Pre-training—Often used to describe the process of training a foundation model to "understand" fundamentals, e.g., of language or images, with the expectation that additional training and testing will be done so the model can be used for a specific task like translation from English to German or facial recognition.

Accuracy—How often a machine is correct compared to an established benchmark in the training and testing data. When you test a new model during the machine learning process, you're often testing its accuracy. Let's say you have your uncle over for dinner and a game of trivia. If your uncle answers "blue" and "round" when you ask him the color of the sky and the shape of the earth, he is accurate. If, after a few glasses of wine, your uncle answers "blue" and "flat" to the same question, his accuracy is suffering. It's important to note that AI accuracy is not a real-world measure and is solely from an AI (not human) perspective. If your uncle was raised by flat-earthers and never learned that the world was round, his answer of "flat" is as accurate as the data he had from his parents. Similarly, if an AI is taught using flawed data, it can be accurate given the data but not empirically, objectively correct when out in the real world.

Precision—How often a machine gives you the same answer. In other words, consistency. When you're testing a new model during the machine learning process, you sometimes ask it the same question multiple times, an opportunity for the machine to give you the same answer (or not). If your uncle gives you a different answer every time you ask him if the world is round, he is not precise. If your uncle always replies "blue" when you ask him if penguins can fly, he is precise but not accurate. In Chapter Four, you'll read about research I've done with Google's AI Overview. Spoiler alert: It has problems with both accuracy and precision.

Reliability—This is a subjective term for the overall performance of AI against human expectations. Highly reliable AI will behave the way we expect it to every time, day or night, out in our real world. The reality is that you often have to decide if the AI is "good enough" for the job you want it to do. Computer scientists and AI companies often want to keep the conversation focused on accuracy, the result of the experiments they control. People like you and me, who have to live with AI in the real world, care only about reliability. The higher the stakes—the more we have to rely on the AI to keep us safe or make us money—the more we expect it to be reliable. I sometimes give up real-world accuracy for precision in higher-stakes situations. For example, I consider the AI in my car to be highly reliable even though its automated lane keeping (stays in one lane by itself) once tried to take an exit that wasn't there. A highway exit had been closed, but new lines had not yet been painted on the road. The old reflective paint lines had been scraped off so they wouldn't mislead drivers at night, leaving a smudged line-like pattern on the road leading off to the right where the exit used to be. My car suddenly tried to swerve right to follow the scraped smudges into the closed exit. Objectively, this was not what I expected and could be considered incorrect in human terms. At first, I was wary and thought about turning off the lane keeping feature. But because the car's AI was consistent, *precise*, and did the same thing it would've done had actual painted lines been there, I saw it as predictable. And predictability is to me an important part of how I perceive reliability. Same decision every time. The AI saw a line-like pattern and followed it. Highly precise. My car could have ignored those remnants of lines, kept going, and arguably have been more objectively correct, but then I wouldn't trust it as much (and it might put me into a guardrail). The Google AI Overview research you'll read about in Chapter Four reveals challenges with both objective truth and precision, but what made me wary the most was that Google AI Overview gave me different answers to the same question. Not precise. Google AI Overview quickly became unreliable to me, so I tend to ignore it.

Transfer Learning—A type of machine learning where you start with a model that has been trained on one data set. You then continue to train the starting model using a different data set. If you've ever benefitted from knowing common Latin root words while studying a foreign language or learning vocabulary in English, you've done your own form of transfer learning. If you know that "aqua" is the Latin word for water, you can transfer that knowledge to learn the words "aquifer" in English, "aquifère" in French, and "agua" in Spanish. Important but not immediately commercially attractive applications of AI have been developed this way. After researchers released some of the first foundation models built from large collections of image data gathered from the internet and our smartphones, medical AI researchers used them as a starting point to teach AI to automatically detect bone fractures. They found that they could get much better results from the relatively small amount of x-ray data they had. The starting model "understood" fundamental characteristics of images like lines, shapes, intensity, and gradient. Those parts of the model transferred to the x-ray model training and didn't have to be learned from scratch from a relatively smaller number of x-rays. The model could "focus" on learning the most important task of identifying fractures in the images.

Generative, Generative AI—A type of AI that generates the next most likely response based on what you give it. You can think of generative as a fill-in-the-blank AI where the blank is at the end of the sentence. Generative AI responds with what is most likely to come next based on the starting point it is given. The starting point is called a "prompt" and can be whatever the AI is designed to accept. Words, a picture, a list of numbers, sound or video recordings can all be the starting point for generative AI to… *generate* what its underlying model has learned is the most likely next piece of information—the response. For example, generative AI can give you the next word in a sentence based on all the words that came before.

When you log into ChatGPT and type:

I like to eat ice

ChatGPT responds with:

cream

That's because in all the text used to train ChatGPT, "I like to eat ice cream" has the highest attention score. In other words, it is the most likely combination. Behind ChatGPT is a pre-trained large language model that in concept contains all of the words in the English language, together with the degree of likelihood that each word will be the next to come after the words before it. You can test this by prompting ChatGPT with the same words but re-arranged into a plain list of words without correct grammar.

For example, when you type:

What is the most likely word
to come next in the sequence
"eat like to ice"

ChatGPT responds with:

cream

This is the core behavior of generative AI. It can get a lot more complicated, but the principle is the same. The "G" in ChatGPT stands for Generative. Note: Not all AI is generative. Another important type of AI is "bidirectional."

Bidirectional AI—A type of AI that produces a response based not only on what is likely to come next, but also on what came before. You can think of bidirectional as AI that is good at understanding things based on the full context of the prompt you give it. Google Gemini is an example of AI that uses a bidirectional model. When you give Gemini the prompt:

What is the meaning of the word "dog" in the sentence "the car broke down and it got so hot the dog let off steam"

Gemini responds with:

In this context, "dog" is slang for something that is of poor quality or unreliable.

On the other hand,
ChatGPT replies to the same prompt with:

the word "dog" most likely refers to an actual dog —as in the animal.

In this example, you can see that the bidirectional AI (Gemini) was better at picking up the semantics of the word "dog" based on the context of the sentence. On the other hand, the generative AI

(ChatGPT) was trained on language data that contained way more mentions of dog the animal than dog the slang word, and it made a prediction based on what it deemed most likely to come *next* (dog, the animal).

Prompt—The starting point that you give AI. Typically, when going back and forth in an interactive "conversation." In school terminology, it's like the essay prompt you respond to with a written document. The word "prompt" came into use with the advent of language-based AI such as ChatGPT. It's really just a new word to describe the input given to an AI tool with the expectation the tool will respond. We typically describe the commands we type into an AI like ChatGPT as our "prompt." If your phone unlocks by showing your face, the image of your face is the "prompt" to the AI on the phone, which responds with "unlock" or "don't unlock." If you're using an AI search tool that searches the web based on a picture you give it, the picture is your "prompt."

Hallucinate—Generative AI will *always* generate a response. No matter what. When the response sounds reasonable but is actually complete nonsense, it is called AI hallucination. By its nature, generative AI will give you the *most likely* response based on all the example data it has learned from. Unfortunately, this response is not guaranteed to be correct.

Prompt Engineering—A (mostly) buzzword for the new-as-of-2022 process of interacting with an AI system to get the most value out of it. Have you done some trial-and-error interaction with an AI? Congratulations! You're a Prompt Engineer! Often people acting as prompt engineers are figuring out how to give an AI the right starting point so it will respond in a useful way and *not* hallucinate. AI systems are not human and have learned by example, so prompt engineers learn how to interact with each (prompt) in a way that "makes sense" given the data the particular AI has been exposed to and the limitations of the tool it is embedded in.

Bot—Slang for any AI that automates a task. "Bot" is often used to describe AI that automates simple tasks in a workflow. For example, a bot might be used to check for billing errors in an accounting system. Another example of a bot is your email spam filter.

Chatbot—Slang for a language-based AI tool that can automatically interact with you in a conversational style. Interaction with modern AI chatbots like OpenAI's ChatGPT is a deliberate feature. The more context the AI has to go on, the more you "chat" back and forth with it, the better it will perform at its given task. At the time of publication, chatbots primarily interact via text or sometimes audio and video. Future chatbots will interact via very realistic video.

Robot—Physical machine that performs a task in the real world. Robots may or may not also use AI for some of their systems. A manufacturing robot that welds car parts probably does not use AI, as it is welding the same parts over and over again. In this case, it is cheaper and better to program the robot to follow a set of predefined procedures. A robotic vacuum cleaner probably uses AI for obstacle detection and avoidance. My car is part AI-enabled robot because it will turn the steering wheel to follow lines painted on the road for its automatic lane keeping safety feature.

Computer Vision—A field of AI and technology that combines cameras with computer systems to observe and interpret the physical world. Computer vision was revolutionized by machine learning and AI. Computer vision has been around for a lot longer than today's AI. Handwriting recognition computer vision systems have read the handwritten and printed addresses on your mail for a long time.

Facial Recognition—A specialized type of artificial intelligence that learns to uniquely identify the faces of human individuals. If your phone unlocks based on an image of your face, it is using facial recognition AI. Facial recognition is part of surveillance, photography, and social media. Do you remember when social media apps automatically recognized and tagged the faces of your friends in pictures? After controversy, one of the biggest apps stopped collecting, processing, and storing faceprints on their servers in 2021. Instead, they and others moved the AI to your phone where it does facial recognition "locally," often to show you advertisements based on the faces of people in your pictures. Researchers have shown as recently as 2024 that these systems are biased in how they link faces to the concepts they use to serve advertisements, such as overly associating the Great Wall of China with Asian women, art paintings with White women, and nudity with White men (West et al., 2024).

Natural Language Processing—A specialized field of AI and technology focused on processing human language for lots of different purposes. Combining natural language processing with computer vision means AI that will interact with humans and the physical world both visually and using human language.

Interactive—A computer system that can respond to human input, typically over multiple back-and-forth cycles. A video game is interactive, as is a chatbot.

Fine-tuning—Teaching a general machine to be better at a more specific task. Or, put another way, the process of starting with a general trained and tested model but then teaching it to be better at something more nuanced. Much fine-tuning is done by starting with a foundation model, say an AI based on a large language model of the English language. The AI is capable of writing thank-you notes for you in a generic style. You could fine-tune the model to be better at responding to prompts with language in a more specific tone or style by doing additional training. You could give it a large collection of letters written in a formal Victorian style, ask it to write a thousand thank-you notes, but only accept the thank-you notes that continued in formal style after a salutation of "Dearest Auntie of Mine." Repeat this enough times, and the model will be better—fine-tuned—for generating formal thank-you notes.

Neural Network—A computer system that mimics the interconnected neurons of your brain. A neuron in your brain takes input in the form of either electrical or chemical signals, processes the input, and if the result of processing rises above a certain threshold, sends either an electrical or chemical signal to the next neuron. A computer neuron is a virtual, digital neuron. It's actually computer code that takes a number as input and processes it by multiplying the input number by a value specific to the virtual neuron (known as a "weight"). If the result rises above a certain threshold, the neuron will pass the number along to the next virtual neuron. Both biological and digital systems learn by creating connected pathways—networks—of many neurons that process information correctly. In machine learning, the cycles of trial-and-error training are used to adjust the weights, the values assigned to each neuron, until the network learns to process information correctly.

Recurrent Neural Network—Recurrent neural networks are good at learning from sequential data like words in a sentence. In concept, they "read" the sentence over and over (recurring) to learn things from it. Let's go back to the "I like to eat ice cream" example. Let's say you want to teach a recurrent neural network to take in a bunch of sentences and tell you which ones are generally positive and happy vs the ones that are negative and sad. Your recurrent neural network will start with the word "I." It "remembers" the word "I" when it looks at the next word "like." It remembers the short phrase

"I like" when it looks at the next word "to." It remembers the short phrase "I like to" when it looks at the next word "eat," and so on until the network has the whole sentence in its memory. After receiving feedback over a few training cycles, it correctly determines that the whole sentence "I like to eat ice cream" reflects a positive sentiment. It then goes on to learn that "my car drives crazy well" also reflects a positive sentiment, even with the idiomatic use of "crazy." Your network is learning that certain one-after-the-other sequences of words indicate positive, happy sentiment. When you give the recurrent network the same words in a different order, "well my car drives crazy," and it guesses negative sentiment, you've taught it that the order of the words matters. A recurrent neural network can learn deeper semantic meaning by building up a representation of sentences one word after the other (recurrent), while never forgetting the words that came before. All this seems intuitive to us humans, but getting a computer to do this was a big deal back around the middle of the first decade of this century.

Convolutional Neural Network—Convolutional neural networks are good at learning from pictures or other grid-like data to find patterns. In concept, they "see" the most important patterns contained in a picture or a grid of numbers. Convolutional neural networks learn from more complex information by breaking it down into layers of simpler information.

Transformer—Transformers are neural networks good at learning from very large amounts of data. In concept, they learn which pieces of data are worth paying attention to, and how those pieces of data are important to each other. This kind of learning can be done in parallel unlike recurrent or convolutional neural networks, so can be scaled up to learn from many, many more examples.

Deep Learning—Using more than two layers of neural networks to approximate the multi-layered structure of the human brain. The first layer takes input, the next layer learns simple patterns, the layer after that more complex patterns, and so on.

Explainable—Artificial intelligence that can demonstrate why it gave a certain response. When AI gets something wrong or hallucinates, we want to know "why." Similarly, we want an explanation when AI is technically accurate given its training data but not objectively, empirically correct from a human standpoint. At this writing, explainability is a "holy grail" of AI. The systems are so complex, with neural networks so dense and interconnected, that from a practical standpoint they are black boxes. It's not currently possible to explain how an AI learned a particular neural network pathway from its training data. The latter point is important because AI are only as "smart" as the data they have been exposed to. Objectively wrong responses indicate a gap in training data that AI developers would like to know about so they can fill it. There is a whole field of research on explainability, and some newer AI are getting better at showing users a loose form of reasoning for their response. But that reasoning is *not* an explanation for exactly how an AI came up with a response based on specific training data. That capability is yet to be discovered.

Bias—When AI responds in a way that shows a preference in one direction that is not objectively correct. For example, an AI taught to predict credit risk that ends up giving lower scores to Black people even if they have the same credit history as White people is exhibiting bias. Bias in AI almost always happens because training data contains bias. In the credit score example, historical data used to train the AI contained reduced scores for Black people originally assigned by people or credit-rating formulas with financial prejudice.

Ethics—Simply put, expecting AI systems and the people who develop and use them to behave according to formal and informal ethical principles. These principles are entirely human and in the eye of the beholder. For example, I may think it is unethical to use AI to pick targets for military strikes, but you may think it is ethical because AI can be less biased or prone to error than humans.

Exercises: Try It Out

- Download Merlin and use Sound ID to learn to identify one type of bird in your backyard.

- Create an account and use this series of prompts with

ChatGPT:

I like to eat…
On a cold day I like to eat…
On a hot day I like to eat…

Notice how the response changes when you give it more to pay attention to. Notice that when it doesn't have much to go on, it responds with a question. This is the interactive nature of chat-based AI. A friend and colleague described working with chat-based AI as like having an eager but inexperienced intern. A good AI intern wants to get it right, so they ask a lot of clarifying questions to be sure it's heading in the right direction. This is deliberate, and a good characteristic. Contrast this with the certainty of Google's AI Overview response. Under what circumstances would you prefer one over the other?

- Dinner party: Do this exercise with a group of people.

Hand out a piece of paper with the same three questions you used with ChatGPT on it.

Ask people to secretly fill in their answers on the piece of paper.

Collect and read everyone's answers, looking for similarities and differences. Then share your observations with your guests.

The stack of papers is a large language model.

You are now a generative pre-trained transformer.

References

Fishbein, Adam R., William J. Idsardi, Gregory F. Ball, & Robert J. Dooling, 2019. Sound Sequences in Birdsong: How Much Do Birds Really Care? *Philosophical Transactions of the Royal Society B.* The Royal Society Publishing. (Retrieved on April 19, 2025, from https://royalsocietypublishing.org/doi/10.1098/rstb.2019.0044)

Galchen, Rivka, 2024. *How Scientists Started to Decode Birdsong*. The New Yorker, October 14.

Gazzaniga, Michael S., 2018. *The Consciousness Instinct: Unraveling the Mystery of How the Brain Makes the Mind.* Farrar, Straus and Giroux.

Kounios, John, & Mark Beeman. 2015. *The Eureka Factor: Aha Moments, Creative Insights, and the Brain.* Independently Published.

McConnell, James V., 1989. *Understanding Human Behavior.* (6th Ed.). Holt, Rinehart, and Winston.

Meta, 2023. *New AI Advancements Drive Meta's Ads System Performance and Efficiency.* Meta. (Retrieved on April 7, 2025, from https://ai.meta.com/blog/ai-ads-performance-efficiency-meta-lattice/)

West, Jack, Lea Thiemt, Shimaa Ahmed, et al., 2024. *A Picture Is Worth 500 Labels: A Case Study of Demographic Disparities in Local Machine Learning Models for Instagram and TikTok.* University of Wisconsin–Madison. ARXiv.org. (Retrieved on April 19, 2025, from https://arxiv.org/pdf/2403.19717)

Wikipedia, n.d. *Wikipedia: Guide to Addressing Bias*. (Retrieved on May 7, 2025, from Wikipedia:Guide to addressing bias - Wikipedia)

Zablotsky, Benjamin, Basilica Arockiaraj, Gelila Haile, & Amanda Ng, 2024. *Daily Screen Time Among Teenagers: United States, July 2021–December 2023*. (Retrieved on April 7, 2025, from Centers for Disease Control and Prevention, National Center for Health Statistics. Products - Data Briefs - Number 513 -October 2024)

CHAPTER 2:
The Rise of Augmented Intelligence

Artificial intelligence can help you do important things you couldn't otherwise do—sometimes by helping you access knowledge and expertise taught to the AI by experts with rare and valuable skills. We call this augmented intelligence.

I serve on the board of a small critical access hospital in a rural area very similar to where I grew up in Central Pennsylvania. I see firsthand the cost to the health of a community of people just like you from lack of ready access to specialized medical skills, compounded by a shrinking healthcare workforce. My blue-sky dream is to bring the right AI in the right way into my hospital to help the dedicated clinicians who do everything possible to care for their patients. An example of what could be in the not-so-distant future: Rib fractures are a strong sign of physical abuse in children under the age of three. These fractures are also very hard to detect. Trained expert radiologists miss them up to two thirds of the time. Simultaneously, far fewer radiologists are entering the workforce, meaning everyone left has to work even faster. Researchers at the University of Michigan and Seattle Children's Hospital are developing AI that may be able to eventually detect rib fractures in toddlers at least as well as a panel of multiple experts reading the same x-rays multiple times (Burkow et al., 2024). If that AI becomes available as a proven tool, it will have been taught the knowledge and practiced skill of a vanishingly small number of expert pediatric radiologists. More children may be helped earlier in their lives if that AI becomes routinely used in emergency rooms that will never, ever be staffed with pediatric experts who can say, "Yes, this baby is being physically abused." An emergency room clinician or the adult radiologist on call in a small community hospital will welcome augmentation—help—from an AI that has been taught very rare skills by experts far away. But augmented AI doesn't have to always be high stakes. We'll get started with a low-stakes example of augmented AI, something just about everyone could use: help with writing in an unfamiliar style.

The day before I started this chapter, my wife, Missy, took her first steps in augmenting her own significant intelligence with AI. Together with a machine, she wrote her first ever advertisement. She works in environmental science and is a talented writer of technical documents, reports, and critical reviews. But ad copy? Never. Furthermore, her approach to new challenges tends to be an endearing progression of "I don't like that, I'll never do it, I tried, it that wasn't so bad, I like it, I'm the best at it." She always ultimately finds success, but in this case, AI helped her through that cycle in record time.

The week before, we had decided to sell advertisements to be read on one of the podcasts I co-host on a subject completely unrelated to AI. We had success selling advertising slots to small businesses that were game, but they couldn't send us what to read "on air." To be clear, our podcast is a low-stakes labor of love that makes no real money. We were charging very little for these ads, not nearly enough to pay a professional to write. So my wife started using ChatGPT to draft advertisements. Actually, what she was using was the collected text from hundreds of thousands of ad copywriters whose knowledge, expertise, and writing had been encoded into the ChatGPT model. She was able to quickly get to a starting point based on their expertise, then add her own voice, humor, and knowledge of the particular small businesses. Artificial intelligence had augmented her skills and intelligence.

Just as the invention of writing scaled the knowledge of the few wise men whose job it was to remember things, and the invention of printing scaled the knowledge of the relatively few who could craft and read hand-lettered manuscripts, AI scales the knowledge of the few who have studied, trained, and gained expertise in writing ad copy and makes it accessible to the many who can now use AI for themselves.

My wife, who did not have the time or inclination to learn to write advertising copy from scratch, used AI to get to a normal baseline or starting point. I use "normal" in the statistical sense here. Artificial intelligence by its nature takes what it learns from specific cases (millions of examples of advertisements) and applies it to a general case it's never seen before. That emphatically does not mean it has the capacity for what we'd recognize as creativity or originality. It learns what advertisements normally look like by reading all the ads that have come before. Convergence on an acceptable model for generating ads will likely mean that model is pretty generic, a statistical representation of an average advertisement. In statistics, the average of a huge data sample like all the ads ever published on the internet is the middle of something called a "normal distribution." In a line graph, a normal distribution looks like an evenly shaped, rounded-off hill. The foothills on the left of the hill are the few really atrocious ads. The foothills on the right of the hill are the few really great ads. And the tall hill in the middle are the many just fine ads. The AI gave her an average, just fine, ad to which she could add her own creativity to produce a unique result. "I was pretty sure I could churn out something," she recalled, "but people have certain expectations for what an ad tells them. I could've read a bunch of advertisements and mimicked someone else's, but I wanted something original. Then it occurred to me that I could use AI to write my ad copy, or to at least get me started."

In this case, she needed an ad for a marina that offers a gas dock, fishing tackle, tour guides, and cottages. She started by typing in "ad copy for marina." The AI spit out some ads, but she felt they were a little too generic. So she cruised around on the marina-in-question's website for a bit and found some specific amenities that they offer and got more specific with her request to ChatGPT. This time, she prompted the AI for "ad copy for fully furnished cottage rentals with river views" and got this:

Experience Serenity: Fully Furnished Cottages with Stunning River Views!

Escape to tranquility in our beautifully appointed cottages, where breathtaking river views and modern comforts combine for the perfect

getaway.

Breathtaking Views: Wake up to panoramic vistas of the river right from your window. Enjoy stunning sunrises and sunsets as you relax on your private deck.

Fully Furnished Comfort: Our cottages come fully equipped with everything you need for a relaxing stay. From cozy bedrooms to spacious living areas, you'll feel right at home in our thoughtfully designed spaces.

This was better, but my wife still felt it was too generic, and not specific to the particular marina or location. So she asked ChatGPT for "ad copy for cottage rentals near great fishing 1000 islands" and got:

Escape to 1000 Islands: Your Ideal Cottage Retreat for Fishing Enthusiasts!

Are you ready to reel in an unforgettable adventure? Discover our charming cottages nestled in the heart of the picturesque 1000 Islands, where pristine waters and stunning scenery await you.

Fishing Paradise: Enjoy direct access to some of the best fishing spots with abundant bass, pike, and trout just steps from your door. Whether you're a seasoned angler or a beginner, our lakes provide the

perfect playground.

Comfortable Getaway: Our well-equipped cottages offer all the comforts of home, including cozy interiors, fully stocked kitchens, and beautiful views to wake up to each morning.

This was better but still lacked key details about the fishing experience. So she took bits and pieces from both responses and wrote the following:

Escape to 1000 Islands and Discover Bill and Jack's Marina—Your Ideal Cottage Retreat for Fishing Enthusiasts!

Are you ready to reel in an unforgettable adventure? Discover our charming, fully furnished and equipped cottages nestled in the heart of the picturesque Fishers Landing, where pristine waters and stunning scenery await you.

Enjoy direct access to some of the best fishing spots on the St. Lawrence River with abundant perch, bass, pike, muskie and walleye just steps from your door. Year after year, the St Lawrence River demonstrates its status as a premier fishing destination in the country by hosting professional, big pay-out fishing tournaments. Come fish with the pros! Whether you're a seasoned angler or a beginner, our river provides the perfect playground.

Bill and Jack's will also assist with all your fishing needs. Gas, ice, fishing license? No problem, we got you. We can also arrange fishing guides upon request!

As you can see, the AI was good at generic ad copy but lacked my wife's first-hand knowledge of the advertiser's business, the details of the locale and what visitors might require, and her human creativity. But together, my wife and a machine produced a compelling and informative ad. The whole was greater than the sum of its parts.

This partnership is a perfect example of augmented intelligence.

So was your use of the Merlin app to learn to identify an unfamiliar bird by its song. Merlin's AI processed a recording of your environment, identified the bird species most likely responsible for the sounds, and then helped you associate the two. Unless you were already an expert birdwatcher, Merlin likely taught you to recognize that bird by its song for the first time. Going forward, your new augmented intelligence means you can identify the bird *and* teach people in your life to identify birds even without Merlin, and the community of ornithologists and birdwatchers who trained Merlin have educated the broader public. Goal met.

So maybe the machines teach us, too. My wife's learning experience with ChatGPT and your new knowledge from Merlin follow the same pattern of learning that we use to teach machines, but flipped around so the lines of *who* is teaching *who* start to blur. Missy made a plan to write an ad with AI and predicted that AI would do it for her (feed-forward). In my wife's case, after a few cycles of giving feedback and adjusting her prompts, the AI had delivered some value but clearly wasn't getting her exactly what she wanted. So she took what *she* had "learned" from the AI and did the rest herself. You can be certain that behind the scenes, OpenAI logged her prompts and repeated interactions with ChatGPT and fed them back into its constant optimization of the underlying AI. This feedback loop is called *continual learning*, and it is a very important factor for long-term success with AI. OpenAI would love to get their hands on what she ultimately wrote but will have to wait to harvest the information from the publicly available podcast, something that happens all the time. More on that later.

These examples show how we benefit from human-AI interaction. Podcast ad copy and bird identification are both relatively low stakes in the immediate sense. Democratizing assessment of child abuse risk from rib x-rays is high stakes. When the stakes are high and a human expert is not readily available, it is important to consider augmentation.

My first very personal experience with high-stakes augmented intelligence caught me by surprise early one morning at a gastrointestinal clinic prior to my first colonoscopy. I wouldn't have known my doctor was using AI during the procedure, except for a serendipitous conversation just before the anesthesia knocked me out. The anesthesiologist had his thumb on the IV control when the gastroenterologist asked me, "So, what do you do?" as part of the scripted distraction. I answered in a weak, hurry-up-and-get-this-over-with voice, "I work in research at the Children's Hospital of

Philadelphia." The doctor said, "Oh, really, what do you research?" To which I answered, "I lead a data and computational program that's getting us ready for AI."

The doctor immediately stopped what he was doing and perked up. "AI? We have AI here! It's called GI Genius, and we're the first practice on the East Coast to use it." Sensing that things were getting sidetracked, the anesthesiologist looked at his watch and then at the gastroenterologist, who nodded and wrapped up our conversation quickly with a "We'll talk later."

True to his word, the first thing my doctor shared when I awoke in the recovery room was his excitement at having used AI to great effect during the procedure. "The AI found a polyp!" he told me. "I would have missed it; it was a little one." I marveled at how an accomplished gastroenterologist, trained to identify, characterize, diagnose, and treat problems of the GI tract, had enhanced his considerable skills by working with a machine. In this case, he explained, the AI watches the same images on the camera during the procedure as the doctor and has been trained to find areas of the colon where a lesion may be located and highlight it on the video screen for the doctor in real time. The doctor can then confirm if there's a lesion and decide what to do about it. The process for training this AI would be just like the training we learned about in Chapter One.

- Domain: Colon cancer screening.
- Task: Identify lesions.

- Metric: Adenoma detection rate better than human alone.
- Data set: A large collection of colonoscopy video recordings.
- Labels: Expert markup of what is and isn't a lesion in the training and testing data videos.
- Model architecture: Convolutional neural network.
- Optimization: Compare expected vs actual classification of lesions.
- Training: Repeat cycles of learning and adjust model until it converges on acceptable precision (classifies the same region in the video as a lesion over and over).
- Testing: Show the trained model data it has never seen before.
- Deployment: Write software and build a device that can show a doctor a circle around a possible lesion on a video screen.
- Continual learning: Collect the doctor's decision on whether or not a region is a lesion and use it to improve the model.

Once GI Genius had been trained, the FDA approved it based on a randomized controlled trial (the gold standard for medical evidence) which showed that doctors doing colonoscopies with the help of GI Genius found thirteen percent more precancerous or cancerous tumors than they found on their own (U.S. Food and Drug Administration, 2021).

Note that augmented intelligence—as opposed to Artificial Intelligence—is collaborative. There isn't anything automatic or push-button about it. Straight-up AI, however, takes people out of the loop. When I drive my car equipped with automated driving assistance, my ability to drive safely at night or in traffic is augmented, but I'm still the one doing the driving. An alert that tells me to stay in the lane is just a suggestion. Contrast this with a fully self-driving car that uses full AI to drive me around while I watch the scenery.

The human-plus-machine system of augmented intelligence puts the *human* in charge of performing the work. The machine just helps. Augmentation helped my wife to create ad copy and improved my doctor's ability to find and remove precancerous lesions. It helped them access expertise that otherwise would not have been readily available.

People, in particular adults, may be the only animals on Earth obsessed with time—having enough time, deciding how to spend time, being on time. When we step out of our daily routine to go on vacation, we usually think about how we want to spend the minutes and hours during those days. Our choice of words—"spending time"—is precisely why augmented intelligence is something that we should all like, seek out, and embrace. Our time is valuable, and just as we do with money, we want to get the most in return for our investment. When we choose to use AI as a means to augment, streamline, or improve the daily tasks and activities that already fill our days, we're using technology to maximize the impact, value, enjoyment, and satisfaction we get from our waking, thinking time. My doctor chose to adopt GI Genius in his practice because he wants to find every single adenoma possible in a given day. Every adenoma found reduces the possibility of cancer in his patients. He was going to get up, go to work, and screen for colorectal cancer eight hours a day no matter what. He was going to make the same amount of money for those hours. But by augmenting his intelligence with an AI tool that still leaves him in charge, he has enhanced what matters most to him, the service he provides for his patients during those hours.

When contemplating augmenting your own skills with AI, you want to think critically and be an informed consumer, as well as an active participant in these human-computer partnerships. Understand how the particular tool you are using came to be. Look beyond the marketing to evaluate what it actually does and does not do after you strip away the hype. Not all AI is created equal, and not all AI is created with your best interests in mind. Remember that AI is as good or as bad as its data, training, deployment, and continuous learning. Your own agency and your ability to question, analyze, and evaluate AI are your most valuable assets in this rapidly changing landscape.

Exercises: Try It Out

Driving

Think: Contrast augmented driving with fully human driving. Do you appreciate AI slamming on the brakes for you or the car behind you in our age of distracted driving thanks to our smartphone use?

Do: If you have a car with advanced driver assistance systems, go for a drive. For liability reasons, I'm not going to suggest you turn your system off! Instead, pay attention to what it does and doesn't do, knowing what you know about how AI is trained, how it works.

Colonoscopy

Think: Contrast augmented polyp detection with fully human or fully autonomous polyp detection. Knowing what you do about human error and the normal imperfections of AI, what are your thoughts on a human and a machine working together?

Do: Use the photo search feature of your phone to find pictures with trees in them. Trees aren't polyps, but you get the idea. Now imagine searching for pictures of polyps all day, every day. Now imagine having AI to help you.

Try reading the paper that published the colonoscopy AI:

> SU 1716 ARTIFICIAL INTELLIGENCE FOR COLORECTAL POLYP DETECTION: HIGH ACCURACY AND DETECTION ANTICIPATION WITH CB-17-08 PERFORMANCE. Repici, Alessandro et al. Gastrointestinal Endoscopy, Volume 89, Issue 6, AB391 - AB392

Write with a chatbot

Augment your own expertise using a chat-based language AI. At the time of publication, ChatGPT by OpenAI or Claude by Anthropic are suitable choices. You're going to do this by first drafting a paragraph about something you know well, then working with AI to improve it.

I'll go first. We heat our house with a wood stove, and I select, cut, split, and stack our firewood. My draft paragraph: "The heat production of a solid fuel wood burning stove is determined by three factors. First, the energy content of the fuel wood. Second, the combustion efficiency of the stove. Third, the transfer of heat from the stove to the living space. Energy content of the fuel wood is affected by the moisture content of the wood. When wood burns, the moisture it contains is converted to steam, taking up energy otherwise available for transfer to the living space as heat. This is why fuel wood should ideally have a moisture content below twenty percent by weight, lower if possible."

Now prompt the chat AI with the following request to edit your paragraph and paste your words in after the colon. "Please make this paragraph better: [paste your paragraph here]" For my paragraph, ChatGPT came back with:

> "*The heat* ***output*** *of a solid-fuel wood-burning stove* ***depends on three key factors: the energy content of the wood, the stove's combustion efficiency, and how effectively the generated heat is transferred to the living space****. The energy content of wood is* ***significantly influenced by its moisture level. When wood contains excess moisture, a portion of the energy released during combustion is used to evaporate water****, rather than to heat the room.* ***For optimal performance****, fuel wood should have a moisture content of less than 20% by weight—****ideally even lower.***"

I bolded some of the changes suggested by the AI. Remember, its suggestions are based on all the text available to it during training—at least the entire internet, including all available digital books. Microsoft may or may not have shared your personal subscription Office document and email content with OpenAI under the terms of their investment in the company. And since 2022, OpenAI has used everything millions of people have typed or pasted into ChatGPT while using it as additional training data, along with our responses for continuous learning.

Now ask the AI to add more detail about one or two aspects of your paragraph. After its first edit, the AI asked me:

> ***Would you like a more technical or more casual version of this?***

I replied:

> "Neither. I would like you to add more detail about different kinds of wood, and more detail about different kinds of wood stoves."

For my paragraph, ChatGPT came back with:

> ***The heat output of a solid-fuel wood-burning stove is determined by three primary factors: the energy content of the wood, the stove's combustion efficiency, and the effectiveness of heat transfer from the stove to the living space. The energy content varies significantly among different types of wood. Hardwoods such as oak, hickory, maple, and beech are denser and generally contain more energy per unit volume than softwoods like pine, spruce, or fir. As a result, hardwoods burn longer and produce more sustained heat, making them a preferred choice for heating. However, regardless of species, the moisture content of***

the wood plays a critical role. Green or freshly cut wood can contain 40–60% moisture by weight, which greatly reduces efficiency. A substantial portion of the energy released during combustion is consumed simply evaporating this moisture. For efficient burning and maximum heat output, wood should be seasoned—air-dried for at least 6 to 12 months—to reduce its moisture content to below 20%, and ideally closer to 15%.

The design and type of wood stove also play a major role in performance. Traditional or non-catalytic stoves rely on high-temperature combustion and manual airflow control, and their efficiency can vary based on how well they are operated. Catalytic wood stoves incorporate a catalyst—typically a coated ceramic honeycomb—that lowers the ignition temperature of the smoke and gases, allowing for more complete combustion and reduced emissions. These stoves tend to offer higher efficiency and longer, more even heat output when properly maintained. Hybrid stoves combine both catalytic and non-catalytic technologies for improved performance across a wider range of operating conditions. Additionally, modern EPA-certified stoves are engineered for cleaner and more efficient combustion, reducing creosote buildup and improving indoor air quality. Finally, heat transfer mechanisms—whether through radiant surfaces, convective air channels, or integrated fans—affect how effectively the heat generated in the firebox is distributed into the room.

An impressive volume of additional detail. How did it do with your paragraph? Did you notice anything you don't agree with? If you did, the point isn't to play "gotcha" and throw the baby out with the bathwater. You keep the good and work on the rest.

You teach the machines! If you did see something you don't consider correct or ideally stated, work with the AI to craft your ideal. Remember the eager but inexperienced intern analogy? Sometimes you have to lead AI by the hand to get the result you want. For my paragraph, I corrected the AI with, "That's not entirely accurate. Catalytic wood stoves have fallen out of favor for polluting more at higher burn rates and for requiring more frequent, expensive maintenance for very little gain in efficiency compared to secondary burn stoves designed to the US EPA 2020 standard. Please update the paragraph accordingly." Your turn with your paragraph.

For mine, the AI did a good job of pulling in more accurate and contemporary information.

It responded, after a polite interjection of:

Thank you—that's a great and important clarification. Here's the revised and corrected version of the paragraph, reflecting the current state of wood stove technology and regulatory standards.

The first paragraph stayed the same, so I won't repeat it. For the second, it made corrections and pulled in relevant up-to-date information:

The design of the wood stove also significantly affects performance. Modern stoves built to meet or exceed the U.S. EPA 2020 standard use advanced secondary combustion technology, which re-burns

> *gases and particulates in a dedicated combustion chamber to extract more heat and drastically reduce emissions. These stoves offer high efficiency with low maintenance and are now considered the industry standard. In contrast, catalytic wood stoves—once popular for their potential to increase efficiency—have fallen out of favor. Although they can achieve cleaner burns under specific low-burn conditions, they tend to pollute more at higher burn rates and require more frequent and costly maintenance. The catalyst component can degrade over time, and its performance depends heavily on proper stove operation. As a result, most manufacturers and users now prefer non-catalytic or hybrid stoves designed to the EPA 2020 standard, which offer cleaner, more reliable, and more user-friendly performance. Lastly, heat transfer methods—whether through radiant surfaces, convective airflow, or integrated fans—impact how effectively heat from the firebox warms the living space.*

Nailed it. How did the AI do with yours after you corrected it? In this exercise, you're using AI to augment your subject-matter expertise with its language model. For generic writing tasks you need to complete quickly, and where you possess all the requisite knowledge to correct the AI if it gets something wrong, this can be quite helpful. You teach the machines!

References

Burkow, Jonathan, Gregory Holste, Jeffrey Otjen, et al., 2024. *High Sensitivity Methods for Automated Rib Fracture Detection in Pediatric Radiograph.* Scientific Reports. (Retrieved on April 21,

2025, from https://www.nature.com/articles/s41598-024-59077-5)

Repici, Alessandro, Nhan Ngo Dinh, Andrea Cherubini, et al., 2019. *Su1716 Artificial Intelligence for Colorectal Polyp Detection: High Accuracy and Detection Anticipation with CB-17-08 Performance*. GIE. (Retrieved on April 21, 2025, from Su1716 ARTIFICIAL INTELLIGENCE FOR COLORECTAL POLYP DETECTION: HIGH ACCURACY AND DETECTION ANTICIPATION WITH CB-17-08 PERFORMANCE - Gastrointestinal Endoscopy)

U.S. Food and Drug Administration, 2024. *FDA News Release: FDA Authorizes Marketing of First Device That Uses Artificial Intelligence to Help Detect Potential Signs of Colon Cancer.* FDA. (Retrieved on April 21, 2025, from https://www.fda.gov/news-events/press-announcements/fda-authorizes-marketing-first-device-uses-artificial-intelligence-help-detect-potential-signs-colon)

CHAPTER 3:
The Industrial AI Revolution

"That's exactly what I want!" My sister-in-law was thrilled to see a picture of a certain type of porch railing that she'd previously had only in her mind's eye. "Thank you so much. Now I can show the architect!"

My daughter grinned. She had just used AI to create a rendering of an architectural detail. She had translated her aunt's meandering description into a series of "prompts" typed into an AI tool which then generated a few possible images. The AI had been taught with the knowledge and practical skill of thousands of architects whose work was published in magazines, books, and on the web. My daughter was able to quickly and easily access and harness the architects' knowledge to accomplish a task without any prior experience or interest in porch architecture and design.

Before AI, knowledge transfer happened one-on-one, passed from an expert to an apprentice, one-to-many, passed from a teacher to a class of students, or one-to-more, passed from an author to readers of a book. Artificial intelligence offers a revolutionary path for the transfer of knowledge. When you teach the machine, it can transfer knowledge and skills from many experts to many, many more users of all backgrounds and skill levels across the globe.

We've been here before. Before the first Industrial Revolution, between roughly 1760 and 1860, an expert shoemaker had exclusive knowledge and skill to make shoes that fit comfortably and worked well. During the Industrial Revolution, inventors transferred the shoemaker's expertise in leather-cutting and sole-stitching to automated machines that could do each task faster and just as, if not more, reliably. After the revolution, shoemakers were out of work, but more people could afford to buy shoes. We are now in the midst of the Industrial AI Revolution—and we can use the lessons of the past to give us an idea of where we are today.

Coal, Iron, and Steam

Coal, iron, the steam engine, and precision machining—that is, the use of machines to make other machines—were the interlocking factors that drove the Industrial Revolution. In 1760, a citizen of Great Britain or the United States likely worked on a farm, possibly growing wheat. Three generations later, their great grandson worked in a factory operating a bread-making machine powered by a steam engine heated by coal. The bread-making machine was made from iron parts cut on a lathe, which was itself powered by a steam engine heated by coal. People in country after country watched their economies industrialize, changing from primarily agricultural to primarily manufacturing. All except Japan, whose Shogunate government managed to keep out the modern world until 1863 when the Choshu Five snuck out of the country to learn the secrets of

Western industry and power in London and returned to overthrow the Shogunate in 1868—proof that it is impossible to ignore or avoid the forward march of human progress.

An analogous change is happening today with AI: Countries with strong knowledge economies—focused on white-collar and professional services—will see their white-collar knowledge worker economies change from all human cognitive labor to a significant amount of AI cognitive labor. Or, if we demand it, primarily human-plus-AI. Artificial intelligence is already changing the work of doctors, lawyers, financial analysts, engineers, computer programmers, anyone who learns a lot about a subject and then uses that knowledge in their work. The more that person currently works alone with information on a computer, the more their work will be affected. People who work with their brains *and* hands will be less affected—plumbers, artists, musicians who perform live. People who empathize, relate, listen, negotiate, and communicate with other people will also be less affected.

Factors of Production

Just as coal, iron, the steam engine, and precision machining drove the first Industrial Revolution, the AI Industrial Revolution is driven by its own factors: nuclear energy, data, graphical processing units, and foundation models.

I grew up on a farm in Pennsylvania near the Three Mile Island nuclear power plant, site of the worst nuclear accident in U.S. history when Unit 2 melted down in late March of 1979. Forty-five years later, in September of 2024, Microsoft ignored the negative association and announced that they had bought all of the electricity that Three Mile Island could produce for the next twenty years. Later in the fall, after Microsoft took the publicity hit, Amazon, Meta, and Google announced that they were all working on their own nuclear electricity generation projects—nuclear energy for computers that run AI.

So why do we need all this nuclear energy? In essence, it's about data, how we store it, and how AI companies process data to train AI. Artificial intelligence training happens in massive electricity-hungry cloud computing data centers sprouting up around the country. What's a cloud computing data center? Starting in the late 1990s, the new economics of the internet made it cheaper to locate your computers wherever you could get the best deal. Electricity and real estate prices became more important than the feel-good comfort of walking down the hall to look at your computer server. Enter the data center boom. A data center is kind of like a modular storage unit facility for your computer servers. Businesses rushed to move their computers from expensive floors in their headquarters to cheap leased space… wherever. Soon companies like Compaq realized they could rent computers in their own data center to other companies without having to box them up and ship them. This became the first generation of "cloud" computing. The phenomenon was described first by young PhD candidate Ramnath Chellappa as a "computer paradigm where the boundaries of computing will be determined by economic rationale rather than technical limits alone" (Biswas, 2025). Marketing people who grew up watching Bob Ross paint happy little clouds decided the executives who signed the checks would swallow this concept if they called it "the cloud" and adopted Ross's imagery in their collateral. Not from the States, younger than me, or had cable when you were a kid? Look up Bob Ross on YouTube.

The smart-aleck phrase, "There is no cloud; it's just someone else's computer" became my mantra when I had to negotiate high-stakes enterprise contracts for my employer with cloud service providers. The cloud service providers needed to be convinced that we weren't going to blindly go along with their convenient buzzwords. I put a sticker of the "There is no cloud…" phrase beneath a sad-faced cartoon cloud on my laptop for the well-intentioned cloud computing company representatives to contemplate while we negotiated terms that would protect our data and our institution.

Amazon Web Services was the first really big cloud computing service provider. Jeff Bezos hated that he had to pay for a mountain of computers to sit idle all year just so his website wouldn't crash when we all ordered books and DVDs at Christmas on Amazon.com. He told his team to figure out how to put them to work the other eleven months of the year, giving rise to even more buzzy terms like "elastic computing." This became the second generation of cloud.

The pendulum swings back as always in history, largely because AI promises to do its thing in real time. If you are a doctor relying on AI to help steer your scalpel during robotic surgery, you're going to want that AI on a computer close by so the camera data going to it and the scalpel-manipulation directions coming back don't take too long in transit. You want those systems connected on your own computer network, or at least on the edge of it. So now we have "edge computing," fancy words for somebody else's computer located down the street instead of somewhere in the "Eastern U.S. Region." A friend works for a company quietly buying up office buildings vacated during the pandemic so they can replace cubicles with computers to run real-time AI for the remaining businesses in the neighborhood where the edge of the AI computer network butts up against the edge of the customers' computer network.

Once you have a reliable supply of electricity for your data center, you need the next major factor: data. In addition to storing more than 17,000 of my emails going back to 2004, Google collects email data from more than 1.8 billion people worldwide, more than 130 million in the U.S. alone, where they are legally allowed to use all of it to train AI. Assuming I'm a typical user, in the U.S. that's 2,210,000,000,000 emails controlled by Google alone. And it doesn't stop with emails, or with Google. The data of the rest of our lives are captured variously by companies like Amazon (retail, publishing, pharmacy), Visa (retail financials), Apple (photos, videos, retail financials), Meta (photos, videos, communications, social activity), JP Morgan Chase (finance, banking), and Epic Systems Corporation (health), along with a host of other quiet but enormous data aggregation companies with benign names like MX, Mobius, and Plaid. All of this data is raw material being used to train AI. With electricity and data secured, it's time to process it.

"We got approval for you to use our graphical processing units!" Bittersweet news from thrilled sales reps of more than one of the cloud computing service providers my employer contracted with. Sweet because we were able to convince mega corporations to allow us to do important but financially dead-end pediatric AI research. Bitter because we'd "won" the chance to pay mid- to high-six figures for the privilege of renting their graphical processing units (GPU) for a few weeks. Graphical processing units are the computers used to teach AI. The "graphical" part of the name confusingly doesn't matter for AI; it's left over from their first major use in video games. At the same time, the CEO of the leading maker of GPU engines that power AI used quarterly financials to proclaim, "The next industrial revolution has begun. Companies and countries are…using GPUs to…build AI factories to produce a new commodity: artificial intelligence" (NVIDIA, 2024a). He drove his analogy home by adding, "The age of AI is in full steam…." The GPU is the new steam engine.

"Wow, it's like a third-year medical student." My colleague was reacting to the results of early research which showed this kind of sci-fi potential when we used large language models made available by big AI companies as a starting point—the foundation. Google, Amazon, Meta, and Microsoft all created massively powerful foundational AI—known as "foundation models"—based on "Attention Is All You Need" the paper discussed in the Introduction to this book. These companies made them available to the marketplace in various ways we'll get into later. Researchers at my previous employer used foundation models to make new machines—previously unattainable AI that, by learning from medical data, could perform common clinical tasks like identifying a disease based on a description of symptoms. Use AI to build new AI. The foundation model is the new machine that makes machines.

The "Attention Is All You Need" authors who invented the Transformer kicked off a chain of events leading to OpenAI's GPT, the first foundation model AI to have a big impact. Nuclear energy, vast reserves of data, and GPUs all existed long before 2017, but foundation model AI—the machines to make machines, or in this case, other AI—did not. A foundation model is characterized not by what it can do directly, but by its potential to make other AI. Or rather, its potential to be "fine-tuned," or further taught to do something useful (see Chapter One). Before the invention of the Transformer described in the "Attention Is All You Need" paper, it didn't matter how many watts of energy, bytes of data, and GPUs you had, it was still prohibitively expensive in *time* to build a foundation model. Really powerful AI took exponentially more time to train with the tools available. Exponential growth means one plus one equals three. When you doubled the amount of data you used to teach AI, you tripled (or more) the amount of time it took to learn. Double your training data over and over so the AI "knows" enough? You're looking at decades or longer.

Ten years ago, at my former employer, we would stare wistfully at large volumes of data, money in the bank to pay the electricity bill, a healthy collection of GPUs, and the ability to buy more. And do nothing. With the tools we had at the time, we'd have to wait years to find out if the machine could learn anything useful. The same was true everywhere. Google, Microsoft, Amazon, Meta, and even the entire country of China had mind-boggling resources of data and dollars to invest. They were already buying GPUs and were ready to buy more. But the one thing they couldn't buy was time.

The Transformer broke the time barrier. The magic of the self-attention mechanism at the heart of the Transformer isn't that it's more accurate (it is). What made it revolutionary was that it didn't require exponentially more time. You could add more data, or teach the machine more lessons, and as long as you also added more GPUs, it would take the same amount of time. This meant experiments could happen in days instead of years. Sitting on the email data of a billion people with billions of dollars burning a hole in your pocket? Call up the GPU salesperson, restart a deactivated nuclear reactor, and with the Transformer, you could train really, really powerful AI in months instead of decades.

The Transformer-based AI was trained to translate between English and German using a well-known standard data set containing four and a half million English-German sentence pairs. A sentence pair is something like "my dog has fleas" matched to "mein Hund hat Flöhe." The Attention team figured out that they could teach their AI three hundred percent more lessons and it would only take fourteen percent longer *without adding any more GPUs*! And if they wanted an even more expert translation AI and used a data set of nine, eighteen, or thirty-six million sentence pairs but kept adding GPUs, it would take the same amount of time.

This meant the corporations and countries who had the data and could buy the GPUs and find enough electricity to run them could teach an entirely new class of AI: foundation model AI capable of making other AI. And that's what happened.

In 2017, Jen-Hsun (Jensen) Huang, the CEO of GPU-maker NVIDIA Corporation, reported annual revenue of $6.9 billion and stated, "We can now see that GPU-based deep learning will revolutionize major industries.... The era of AI is upon us." By 2023, all the big AI companies had trained foundational large language models. In fiscal year 2023, Mr. Huang reported revenue of $26.97 billion and said, "AI is at an inflection point, setting up for broad adoption reaching into every industry" (Choe & Parvini, 2023; NVIDIA, 2023).

NVIDIA, the company that makes GPUs that power AI, saw its revenue grow four hundred percent in the five years that included a global pandemic (Global Macro Monitor, 2024). Microsoft, Google, Amazon, and Meta all bought as many GPUs as possible in a race to build the machines that make machines for the coming industrialization of AI.

NVIDIA announced "partnerships" with the AI companies in this time period. Their biggest customers became something more. NVIDIA also tried and failed to buy their competitor chip designer Arm Holdings for $40 billion. The U.S. Federal Trade Commission squashed the deal with a lawsuit. Not to be deterred, NVIDIA went on the open market and quietly acquired hundreds of millions of dollars of Arm stock and announced new partnerships with Arm (Turner & Bloomberg, 2024).

Just as coal, iron, steam engines, and precision machine tools combined to industrialize human production work, nuclear energy, data, graphical processing units, and foundation models are combining to rapidly industrialize human knowledge work. Rapidly because instead of a century-long evolution driven by small entrepreneurs and inventors, AI industrialization is being driven by some of the wealthiest corporations on the planet.

Big AI

"Big Tech" companies are likely secretly happy with this moniker and tolerate its sometimes negative associations. They love it when a politician or an activist rails against "Big Tech" for controlling internet searches, computer operating systems, and social media. That means we're looking the other way while the same companies quietly go about the business of harvesting our personal data and building up the capital to turn our data into profitable AI. The truth is that Big Tech has actually become Big AI.

The first Industrial Revolution played out over a hundred years, from 1760 to 1860. Change was driven by inventors, entrepreneurs, small, and then mid-sized, businesses in every community. The inventive shoemaker dreamed up a mechanized leather cutting machine. He partnered with the enterprising blacksmith next door to buy an early lathe to make his machine. They went in together on a shop next to the flour mill so they could run both their machines off the steam traction engine the innovative miller had bought to replace his water wheel. The shops sat next to a river full of barges shipping coal from independent mines, steel from small foundries. Now able to produce a larger volume of quality shoes, the shoemaker hired a farmer to run the leather-cutting machine in the afternoon after he had tended the fields. He sold shoes at a lower price, including a pair to the previously barefoot daughter of the farmer. The blacksmith trained the first machinist in the state to make leather-cutting machines which the partners then sold to shoemakers in nearby towns. There weren't any big companies, and the truly private corporation wasn't legal until politics and business conspired in the 1890s. Our cooperative of entrepreneurial small businesses could thrive. The farmer paid off a loan and hired a hand. His daughter went to school in the spring instead of planting corn. Life got better as the whole pie grew and more citizens got a slice. But there were limits to what could happen at this scale.

After this revolutionary period, large corporations began to emerge, at least in the U.S. Innovative, driven businessmen created new corporate and financial strategies with the goal of maximizing profit, often by beating the competition with a better product at a better price. Conglomerates in shoemaking equipment (United Shoe Machinery), oil (Rockefeller), steel (Carnegie), railroads (Stanford's Central Pacific), electricity (J.P. Morgan's General Electric), and tobacco (Duke's American Tobacco) rolled up their respective sectors. At their best, these conglomerates created economies of scale that allowed them to invest in innovation, efficiency, and the workforce, ultimately improving quality of life for more citizens. At their worst, the conglomerates put competitors out of business and did *not* invest in innovation, efficiency, and the workforce, ultimately leading to real and perceived economic injustice. Fifty years after the entrepreneurial frenzy of the Industrial Revolution, in some sectors, a very few businesses controlled all or most factors of production and sales in their industry. John D. Rockefeller's Standard Oil owned the oil fields, drilling companies, refineries, and effectively the railroads (through exclusive freight contracts), pipelines, heating oil distributors and gasoline service stations. Standard Oil's relentless pursuit of efficiency drove down the cost of oil nearly tenfold by the early 1900s. The first industrialists were also politically active, as they sought to influence regulatory and tax policy to their benefit, much as today's corporations hire lobbyists to advance their interests with whatever party is in power.

The political influence of Rockefeller and his contemporaries is best illustrated by the rapid evolution of corporate law. In the 1880s, Leland Stanford obtained "personhood" for his Southern Pacific Railroad, which established the precedent that a corporation has the same protection against discrimination as a human under the Fourteenth Amendment. In Stanford's case, the discrimination was a special tax on railroad property enacted by the State of California (Ballotpedia, n.d.). Not what the Fourteenth Amendment was meant to protect when it was enacted after the Civil War to protect the rights of freed slaves. Personhood gave corporations special protections, but they were still subject to strict controls on their power by the state legislatures that chartered them. J.P. Morgan created a permissive home for corporations by hiring a lawyer to rewrite New Jersey's corporate law to remove restrictions meant to prevent abuse of power. The changes were happily adopted by the governor and legislature in return for franchise taxes. Indeed, after Ohio broke up Rockefeller's Standard Oil Trust under state law, the oil conglomerate moved to New Jersey to take advantage of the state's enabling corporate laws. In the 1890s, public (and competitor) backlash against industrialists and their political influence, as well as real and perceived anti-competitive practices, brought new federal antitrust laws and ultimately a period of enforcement that resulted in the breakup of many monopolies, including Standard Oil in 1911 (Oller, 2019). But the industrialists hadn't gained power until the *end* of the first Industrial Revolution, after decades of improvement in standard of living, life expectancy, access to education, and other measures of life, liberty, and the pursuit of happiness.

Artificial intelligence industrialization went straight to conglomerate. Arguably, Big AI didn't even experience the speed bump of an extended or widespread entrepreneurial phase, given that it already had twenty years of momentum. Big AI rapidly invested enormous amounts of capital to consolidate control over factors of AI production, and wielded political influence to increase profits. By early 2025, Microsoft controlled the data of 400 million Microsoft 365 users (iron); had acquired a nuclear energy plant (coal); was in multiple financial relationships with a key GPU supplier, NVIDIA (steam engines); and had a $13 billion stake in OpenAI's GPT foundation models (machines to make machines). Microsoft, NVIDIA, BlackRock (the world's largest investment company), and MGX (the United Arab Emirates' sovereign wealth AI fund) are in a partnership to invest $80 to $100 billion in new data centers exclusively for AI controlled by Microsoft (BlackRock, 2025). Meanwhile, Google controls the data of 1.5 billion Gmail users (not to mention the data from YouTube and Google Photos), has built its own version of the GPU, is developing multiple nuclear energy projects and has its own foundation models plus a $2 billion stake in the foundation models of another wealthy AI company called Anthropic. Amazon controls data from more than 500 million Alexa devices plus the data of more than 350 million retail customers and the connected data of more than 200 million Prime users, has its own foundation models plus an $8 billion stake in Anthropic's models, buys as many of NVIDIA's GPUs as it's allowed to, while making its own GPUs, and is invested in multiple nuclear energy projects. Meta controls the data of the 3.9 billion people who use its apps every month, is in a partnership with AMD (an NVIDIA competitor) to design and build GPUs to install in its new $10 billion AI data center in Louisiana, and has its own foundation models.

As far as political influence goes, the inaugural U.S. National AI Advisory Committee (NAIAC), established by a law passed in 2020 and first convened in 2022, is made up of a who's who of delegates from NVIDIA, Google, Microsoft, Amazon, Anthropic, and others, along with academics and policymakers (U.S. Department of Commerce, 2022). Big AI is giving the advice. The CEOs of the Big AI companies exert more influence when they meet with presidents and presidents-elect of both parties in private, because AI is positioned as a national security issue. Mr. Huang from NVIDIA stated in 2024 that "Countries have awakened to the importance of developing their national AI and infrastructure." His use of the plural "countries" and the word "national" is in keeping with a sometimes arms-race response from elected officials around the world. Which certainly won't hurt business.

Industrial and corporate history is context for the emerging AI industry. AI will change our lives and the lives of our children and grandchildren just as the industrialization of manufacturing changed the lives of our great-great-grandparents. The AI produced by corporations is already changing the nature and value of human cognitive labor. Governments around the world are wrestling with novel policy questions, often with AI corporations in the room. Intertwined political and corporate interests are a nonpartisan phenomenon. Left, right, red, blue, or purple, it is our job as citizens, voters, and consumers to make informed choices that promote benefit and minimize harm of AI. My use of the term Big AI does not imply a negative, just as the use of the term Big Three to describe the major U.S. automakers is not a negative. Modern AI requires a scale of production that only very large corporations or governments can support (for now). Big is not necessarily bad for the individual citizen or society as a whole. Big is less likely to become bad when you have a sense of agency and are an active participant in the change brought by AI. You can be a driver of change. You can have an active role in this new, latest industrial revolution. And that role starts with your data. You teach the machines.

Follow The Data

The most important technology in human history since the printing press relies entirely on your data. When AI improves enough from learning from you and everyone around you, you will be more likely to pay for what it can do. Data is an asset that increases in value as it grows in size, and the big AI companies have been working toward this moment for decades. Ever hear the adage, "If it's free, there's a catch"? For years, I assumed that Gmail, Facebook, and Amazon's one-day delivery were free because "Big Tech" wanted to target me with ads. It was true. But only partially. What they really wanted was my data. Yes, with my data, they could learn of my interest in Iceland and sell a premium targeted ad to Icelandair. But the real money was in banking my data and the data of hundreds of millions of other people, because they knew value depended on volume when it came to training AI. Between 2010 and 2015, the data representing your digital life became a corporate asset with future value to train AI. It didn't cost much to store in the cloud, so collecting ever and ever larger volumes was a safe, long-term bet that, at a certain point, it would be feasible to use your data to industrialize AI. You teach the machines.

As discussed previously, when you read and agree to the Microsoft Service Agreement and Privacy Statement, it's clear that by clicking "I accept," you are allowing Microsoft to use your data to do anything permissible by law.

An excerpt follows, accessed on April 22, 2025:

> *b. To the extent necessary to provide the Services to you and others, to protect you and the Services, and to improve Microsoft products and services, you grant to*

Microsoft a worldwide and royalty-free intellectual property license to use Your Content

As you can see, per the Service Agreement, you "grant to Microsoft a worldwide and royalty-free intellectual property license to use Your Content." And if you follow the links to the Microsoft Privacy Statement, it's clear they have a royalty-free license to share your data with third parties like, say… OpenAI. That means the sentences and paragraphs I type into Microsoft 365 Word today could find their way into the dataset used tomorrow to train the next generation of ChatGPT. They are forthright enough in their privacy statement to come right out and say that:

> *As part of our efforts to improve and develop our products, we may use your data to develop and train our AI models.*

To be clear, this degree of transparency means that Microsoft is behaving *well* under the U.S. laws to which I'm subject. And it doesn't just relate to content you type in Word. The "Services" referenced in this agreement are, at the time I'm writing this, an ever-expanding list of one hundred and thirty-eight Microsoft products from Excel (yes, your retirement spreadsheet) to Teams to your XBox.

OpenAI's GPT-3, the AI that blew all our minds, was trained on a large volume of unrestricted, publicly available data. Microsoft wrote OpenAI a check for $13 billion in 2020 possibly because they knew how much more "proprietary" data Microsoft had and were going to continue to acquire, and Microsoft was certain that they could return hundreds of billions of dollars more by combining your data with OpenAI's technology.

But it isn't just Big AI companies. I got an email from my bank, Wells Fargo, telling me that by continuing to use their banking services, I agreed to changes in their Online Access Agreement.

The summary of changes includes a paragraph on their use of my information, accessed on April 22, 2025:

> *Updated Section 17(b) (Privacy and Use of Information: Acknowledgements and Agreements) to (i) clarify that your communications with us may be analyzed and processed (potentially through automated means), and may be shared with our service providers and other third parties, in accordance with our privacy policy and applicable law...*

The "potentially through automated means" indicates AI. The "shared with our service providers and other third parties" means practically whoever they want, and I'll never know. Within the law, of course.

A quick word on privacy: We in the U.S. have a general sense that we have a good faith expectation, if not a right, to privacy, that our data will be kept private. That's why it's news (and a hit to share prices) when a company has a data breach. And if data is shared, we expect that our name and identifying details will be removed, making it anonymous or deidentified. There is no explicit protection of this expectation or right in the Constitution, even though the Supreme Court has inferred it from many of the ten amendments that make up the Bill of Rights. But U.S. laws and court decisions have trouble keeping up. Because there is no right protected by law, we choose to give our data up under contractual terms of use that almost nobody reads. And we are also surprised when we find out that a company is doing something… creepy with our data. Without going into the details, please accept for now that, for example, if a company has every email you've ever written, it doesn't matter if your name has been stripped from the email or not. The combination of unique information in those emails is easily linked to your identity. Claims that your data are stored without your identifying information, while technically true, are now irrelevant to practical privacy. When you see them, recognize that, for all practical purposes, they remain as a tonic to help you feel more comfortable with the idea that the book you're writing is being used wholesale to train AI, share with third parties, and make money under a royalty-free license. Microsoft actually does a pretty good job of *not* claiming to anonymize your data in the terms I've seen. At least they're more transparent!

It may seem like I'm picking on Microsoft, but it's all of the Big AI companies. And for now, everything these companies do with your data is completely legal. Is it right? Wrong? Creepy? That's for you to decide. But you know what else was thoroughly wrong and creepy, yet legal at the time it was done? Harvesting cells from a woman named Henrietta Lacks without her knowledge and then making billions of dollars from them.

The Story of Henrietta Lacks

On October 4,1951, at Johns Hopkins Hospital in Baltimore, a thirty-one-year-old woman named Henrietta Lacks died of complications from tumors growing all over her body. In her 2006 book *The Immortal Life of Henrietta Lacks*, author Rebecca Skloot writes about the injustice and institutional racism that led to a death that might have been avoided or at least made less painful. She also writes about how a researcher took cancer cells from Mrs. Lacks, without her knowledge or consent, that proved to be the first "immortal" cells to grow reliably in a test tube. The researcher and Johns Hopkins gave these cells away for free to scientists all over the world who used them to study cancer and many other diseases. Eventually, third parties like pharmaceutical and biotechnology companies acquired the cells and used them to make drugs and other biological products.

The book is about much more than what happened with these cells, and I encourage you to read it or watch the movie based on Mrs. Lacks's story. I also encourage you to consider possible parallels between Mrs. Lacks's cells and your own personal data.

In her afterword, Ms. Skloot writes:

> *Beyond simply knowing their tissues are being used*

> *in research, some tissue-rights activists believe donors should have the right to say, for example, that they don't want their tissues used for research on nuclear weapons, abortion, racial differences, intelligence, or anything else that might run contrary to their beliefs. They also believe it's important for donors to be able to control who has access to their tissues, because they worry that information gathered from tissue samples might be used against them.*

If we rewrite this paragraph, swapping the word *tissue* for *data*, we get:

> *Beyond simply knowing their* ***data*** *are being used in research, some* ***data****-rights activists believe donors should have the right to say, for example, that they don't want their* ***data*** *used for research on nuclear weapons, abortion, racial differences, intelligence, or anything else that might run contrary to their beliefs. They also believe it's important for donors to be able to control who has access to their* ***data****, because they worry that information gathered from* ***data*** *samples might be used against them.*

This certainly seems reasonable to me. But it's wishful thinking at this point in the U.S. Even with sensitive data like your health records and financial information, healthcare providers are allowed to do whatever they want with your data so long as something called an Institutional Review Board determines that it would not be feasible to ask you for your permission and weighs in on the risks and benefits. Next time you go to the doctor, pay attention when you're asked to sign a digital pen pad acknowledging that you've read and understand the Notice of Privacy Practices. From a legal perspective, that signature means you have provided consent for your data to be used in any way allowable on the Notice and by law.

Does the government have anything to say about this? In short, in the U.S., as of May 2025: No. Maybe with some exceptions in California. You have to look elsewhere for another model. The European Union passed legislation called the General Data Protection Regulation, which requires more transparency and control of data for citizens of the EU. As a result, Amazon's terms governing your data (including the use of Alexa in your home) are 3,600 words in the United States and 8,700 in Germany.

Does this all seem like… a lot? It is. I work in the AI sector, and in some ways, I knew all of this before I sat down to write this chapter. But seeing it all laid out on the page in black and white is sobering. We all need to be savvy and protect ourselves.

Exercises: Try It Out

If you have a Google account:

- Log in and search "good present for my [best friend? sister? brother? spouse/partner?]
- Log out and do the same search. Do you see anything different?

- Look up and compare a data policy in the EU to a data policy in the U.S. for the same company.
- Next time you see your doctor, ask for a copy of the notice of privacy practices that you "acknowledge you've received" when you sign the little digital signature pad or complete the online check-in.
- Search a major national news website for "new nuclear reactor" or "proposed nuclear reactor." Look to see who the investors and backers are.
- Read NVIDIA's last couple of earnings reports, especially commentary from company leadership. Dig and find a transcript of the earnings call and see what questions analysts ask and how NVIDIA responds.

References

Ballotpedia, n.d. *Santa Clara County v. Southern Pacific Railroad Company*. (Retrieved on April 22, 2025, from Santa Clara County v. Southern Pacific Railroad Company - Ballotpedia)

Biswas, Sourya, 2025. *History of Cloud Computing: A Journey of Innovation and Future Prospects*. Cloud Tweaks. (Retrieved on May 8, 2025, from History Of Cloud Computing: A Journey Of Innovation And Future Prospects)

BlackRock, 2025. *Press Releases: BlackRock, Global Infrastructure Partners, Microsoft, and MGX Welcome NVIDIA and xAI to the AI Infrastructure Partnership to Drive Investment in Data Centers and Enabling Infrastructure*. (Retrieved on April 22, 2025, from AI Infrastructure Partnership | BlackRock)

Choe, Stan, & Sarah Parvini, 2023 (Updated January 28, 2025).

Nvidia Faces a Reckoning as Chinese Upstart Raises Questions About Wall Street's Darling. AP. (Retrieved on April 22, 2025, from Nvidia faces a reckoning as Chinese upstart raises questions about Wall Street's darling | AP News)

Global Macro Monitor, 2024. *NVIDIA's Stunning 400% Growth in Data Center Revenue*. Macromon. (Retrieved on April 22, 2025, from NVIDIA's Stunning 400% Growth In Data Center Revenue | Global Macro Monitor)

Hindle, Brooke, & Steven Lubar, 1986. *Engines of Change: The American Industrial Revolution, 1790–1860.* Smithsonian Institution Press.

Knipprath, Joerg, 2017. *Justice Stephen J. Field (1816–1899)*. Constituting America. (Retrieved on April 22, 2025, from Justice Stephen J. Field (1816-1899) – Constituting America)

McCarthy, Eugene, 2023. *Corporate Law, Business Schools, and White-Collar Crime*. St. Louis University Law Journal, 67. (Retrieved on April 22, 2025, from https://scholarship.law.slu.edu/cgi/viewcontent.cgi?article=2330&context=lj)

Microsoft, 2024. *Microsoft Services Agreement*. (Retrieved on April 22, 2025, from Microsoft Services Agreement)

NVIDIA Corporation, 2017. *Newsroom: NVIDIA Announces Financial Results for Fourth Quarter and Fiscal 2017*. (Retrieved on April 22, 2025, from NVIDIA Announces Financial Results for Fourth Quarter and Fiscal 2017 | NVIDIA Newsroom)

NVIDIA Corporation, 2023. *Press Release Details: NVIDIA Announces Financial Results for Fourth Quarter and Fiscal 2023*. (Retrieved on April 22, 2025, from NVIDIA Corporation - NVIDIA Announces Financial Results for Fourth Quarter and Fiscal 2023)

NVIDIA Corporation, 2024a. *Computer Industry Joins NVIDIA to Build AI Factories and Data Centers for the Next Industrial Revolution*. (Retrieved on May 8, 2025, from Computer Industry Joins NVIDIA to Build AI Factories and Data Centers for the Next

Industrial Revolution | NVIDIA Newsroom)

NVIDIA Corporation, 2024b. *NVIDIA Announces Financial Results for Third Quarter Fiscal 2025*. (Retrieved on April 22, 2025, from NVIDIA Announces Financial Results for Third Quarter Fiscal)

Oller, John, 2019. *White Shoe: How a New Breed of Wall Street Lawyers Changed Big Business and the American Century*. Dutton.

Skloot, Rebecca, 2011. *The Immortal Life of Henrietta Lacks*. Crown.

Turner, Nick, & Bloomberg, 2024. *Nvidia Tried and Failed to Buy Arm for $40 billion in 2020, but It Just Reported a Stake Worth $147.3 Million*. Fortune. (Retrieved on April 22, 2025, from Nvidia discloses $147.3 million stake in Arm | Fortune)

U.S. Department of Commerce, 2022. *U.S. Department of Commerce Appoints 27 Members to National AI Advisory Committee*. (Retrieved on April 22, 2025, from U.S. Department of Commerce Appoints 27 Members to National AI Advisory Committee | U.S. Department of Commerce)

Wells Fargo, n.d. *We Are Updating Our Online Access Agreement*. (Retrieved on April 22, 2025, from We Are Updating Our Online Access Agreement)

CHAPTER 4:
Side Effects and Pitfalls

> *The vitality of democracy depends on popular knowledge of complex questions.*
> —S.S. McClure

Writing this chapter, in which I present what many see as the "bad news" of AI, was simultaneously depressing and encouraging. Depressing because, at the time I'm writing, a relatively small number of large corporations are deploying AI into our lives as fast as possible. And it's all pretty opaque. Encouraging because major change from AI has yet to happen. There is time for you, me, and our loved ones to shape change for the better. To be a driver, not a passenger. You teach the machines.

The words came easily, but I became dejected while building a point of view from facts, interpretation of facts, and theories to explain what is not publicly available. There's a lot that is behind a curtain. You intuitively know AI will reshape your life. Simultaneously, you don't understand how. You can be overwhelmed by this combination of knowledge and uncertainty. I became overwhelmed and depressed as I considered the negative implications of this new technology accelerated by a generational deployment of capital, concentration of wealth, erosion of education, disruption of jobs, and shifting global security. My editor stepped in and coached me to focus on the specific, the actionable. Always good advice.

In this chapter, you'll see my editorial point of view come through, so be a critical reader. Know that I remain an AI optimist, so I try to balance points of potential doom with action you can take. The legal and publicity departments at the companies I discuss may argue with what I write. In many ways I am rooting for these same companies to succeed. They're doing incredibly difficult and historical work. I invite them to help make a second edition of this book even better. But a corporation is legally obligated to seek one simple outcome: Maximize profit. The reality is that better *human* outcomes depend entirely on you, me, your parents, your kids, the values we teach, and the decisions we make. I try to give you at least some idea of how you can be part of the solution to the problems I discuss. But if there is one thing you should take away from this chapter, it is that you need to prepare for the unknown. Prepare by taking stock of your first principles. Mine are "Be nice. Get stuff done. Make things less crappy." Medical professionals go with "Above all, do no harm." What are yours? We're in for a lot of change, currently driven by corporations in effect experimenting and gambling with our economy and lives. Anchor yourself with clear principles that can steer you when unexpected change from AI hits. Humans are built to adapt. We're going to do a lot of it in the coming decades.

A side effect is an unintended bad thing you experience from doing something else. A headache from taking antibiotics, maybe. A pitfall is a known hazard you allow yourself to fall into. A headache from drinking too much.

An unintended side effect in the world of AI? Depending on your point of view, the relative reduction in investment in renewable energy in favor of investment in nuclear energy. A corresponding pitfall "we" knowingly step into with more nuclear energy? The coming increase in solid nuclear waste stored on site at nuclear energy plants, at least in the U.S., because we as a society, represented by the people we've elected for the past twenty years, are politically unable to pull off long-term consolidated storage. See Yucca Mountain.

But even this side effect can have a balancing upside. Investment in nuclear energy is bringing real innovation in the form of more efficient, cleaner nuclear reactors. And if you consider a reduction of investment in renewable energy a side effect because of climate change, then you have to consider that use of nuclear energy is better than burning more fossil fuels.

Regrets

In May of 2023, Geoffrey Hinton resigned from Google. Eleven years earlier, he and his team had built the first neural networks at the University of Toronto. They founded a company that was quickly bought by Google for $44 million. Dr. Hinton went to work for Google to advance the research. Ten years later, at the time of his resignation, he stated that a part of him regrets his life's work (Kleinman & Vallance, 2023).

The main inventor of modern AI regrets his life's work. Sit with that.

Geoffrey Hinton, an insider's insider, knows AI as much as or more than anyone else on the planet. He resigned from Google, the original industrial AI company, so he could speak freely about the hazards he sees at Google and beyond.

Dr. Hinton was a hero of sorts to me and my colleagues working in health AI long before he stood on principle. He worked for decades against conventional wisdom to prove the power of computer programs modeled on how neurons in the brain learned skills by analyzing data. After Google joined the AI arms race started by Microsoft's investment in OpenAI in 2020, he became concerned that his company and its competitors were moving too fast, given the stakes for the rest of us.

He grew concerned that rapid proliferation of "fake" AI-generated text, video, and voice would make it impossible for us to know what was true. He grew very concerned that we would lose our jobs and incomes as AI replaced or cheapened the labor of paralegals, analysts, call center workers, writers, lawyers, financial experts, doctors, nurses, engineers, and software programmers. He became very, very concerned with the weaponization of AI into autonomous killing machines. Dr. Hinton wasn't alone. Even before his resignation, over a thousand technology leaders called for a moratorium on training advanced AI. They wanted time to understand possible side effects and work to minimize the harm of known pitfalls.

Too late. A year later, Microsoft effectively bought a nuclear power plant. Bezos, Musk, Pichai, Nadella, Altman, and Cook—the modern-day Stanfords, Rockefellers, Dukes, and Morgans—couldn't risk someone else winning. Shareholders demanded returns. Not just some mysterious shareholder "other," but each and every one of us invested in the tech-heavy U.S. stock market. Google ignored the call for a moratorium and rolled out AI-generated search answers at the top of their search page.

Change

Side effects and pitfalls flow naturally from change. Artificial intelligence is a miles-long freight train of change driven by hundreds of billions of dollars. You, I, your parents, your kids are locked in a stalled car at the railroad crossing. Artificial intelligence is changing or will soon change how you write a report for work, an essay for school, improve your firm's profits by automating junior associate work, drive a car, identify mental health problems, deny insurance coverage, get your electricity, trust or mistrust information, experience art and entertainment, and fight wars.

Which changes will bring side effects? Which have known

pitfalls? Wouldn't it be nice to take a minute and think about it? Like the experts wanted "way back" in 2023?

Practical AI went from invention to industry in ten years. Neural networks emerged in 2012 and became scalable five years later with the Transformer in 2017. Corporate Industrialization into a financially and politically intertwined handful of corporations took five years between 2017 and 2022. What took more than one hundred years for the first Industrial Revolution took only ten for AI. As I write this in 2025, the Big AI companies are in a race to remake the knowledge economy. How many quarterly earnings reports do you think they're willing to produce before they can report returns to their impatient investors? The leadership and shareholders of the Big AI companies in the U.S. alone are betting hundreds of billions of dollars that they can return trillions as fast as possible. Look at the concentration of wealth in the hands of the leaders of these companies and their investors. Again, they have a legal obligation to maximize profits. Do you think they're truly, fundamentally interested in growing the whole pie?

AI has never happened before. It went from theory to practice in ten years. The economy of AI as it's currently playing out means the richest corporations control the means of production right up front. Contrast this with the rise of the internet and World Wide Web. Public communication protocols arose out of publicly funded research and were taken up by anyone with a computer and a phone line. Web browsers and server software freely available to all allowed people to use their existing phone lines to build their own websites at home. Internet service providers sprung up at the local town level. The web quickly became of, by, and for the people.

Artificial intelligence is on the opposite track. The Big AI corporations possess barely comprehensible financial power. They use real and perceived expertise to gain political influence based in part on a popular assumption that AI is central to national security. Multiple sessions of Congress and multiple presidents have come and gone with no new regulatory guardrails in the United States. Hundreds of billions of dollars already at stake demand returns. It's as if Gutenberg and the early printing press experts weren't chased out of Mainz during an unrelated religious power struggle so the printing press could disseminate organically. It's as if, instead, they formed a corporate combine, an industrial business group that held absolute power over the manufacture and use of the printing press. It's as if they cozied up to and contributed hundreds of millions in dark money to the most powerful leaders in Europe of every party to insulate themselves from regulation and maximize profits. It's as if they relaxed standards on control of misinformation in the books they printed to gain influence. It's as if human knowledge and skill were captured, transferred to others, and used for good and bad in entirely unprecedented new ways by corporations concerned only with winning the trillions of thalers at stake.

We're at the beginning of rapid societal, cultural, and economic change directed by profit. Maybe it'll be fine. Let's look at puppies and covet the lives of others on social media instead of worrying.

With that rant out of the way, it's time to buck up and be part of the solution. "You teach the machines" could mean you're passively milked of your data and money. Or it could mean you're in front of the room, directing and taking charge. You're the windshield, not the bug. You teach the machines.

Dr. Hinton's Fears

Geoffrey Hinton gives us a framework for the first major known side effects and pitfalls we'll discuss: misinformation, job loss, and killer robots (the use of AI in war). In my professional life, I've spent a lot of time working on the first two, albeit focused on the health sector. Thankfully, I've never met a killer robot in a "hot war" but have had direct experience with scary "cold war" AI threats and harm.

1. Misinformation

Consider the same internet search three months apart for "European causes of accidental death" using the Google search page, which around ninety percent of us do globally. I have screenshots of everything to prove this actually happened.

On November 19, 2024, Google's AI Overview listed the causes as:

- road traffic injuries

- drowning
- falls
- burns
- poisoning

It stated that "road crashes are the most significant cause," which I took to mean this was a rank ordered list.

On January 27, 2025, Google's AI Overview reordered and changed the causes to:

- road traffic accidents
- falls
- drowning
- poisoning
- work-related accidents.

In three months, falls overtook drowning, and burns dropped from the list to be replaced by work-related accidents.

Which is true? Turns out neither, according to my own research on the website of EuroStat, the statistical office of the European Union, which Google *seemed* to point to as a source for both AI Overview results. A half hour spent with the freely available data there revealed the causes, in order of decreasing death rate (deaths per 1,000 people), to be:

- falls
- other
- transportation accidents

- poisoning
- drowning

"Other" includes a scary list of things like struck by falling objects, exposure to animate mechanical forces, and overexertion.

Generative AI by its very nature will always give you (generate) an answer, an image, a song, a diagnosis. Truth doesn't matter in subjective "eye of the beholder" circumstances like composing an advertisement, and you need a starting point. Truth matters in the realm of life-and-death facts and figures. Say you're a busy European legislator and need a sound bite for your speech about accidental death. You draft the speech with results from the top of the search page and understandably miss the small-font disclaimer that "Generative AI Is Experimental" or "AI responses may include mistakes." This is what Dr. Hinton was talking about when he resigned. People lose sight of what is really true with unreliable or manipulated AI as an intermediary.

You'll hear the term "hallucination" thrown around when AI presents something that you figure out is straight up wrong. I prefer "drunk uncle" because I'd rather think of AI in the context of the example above as an inebriated relative spouting off malarkey and conspiracy theories. Hallucination is a kind word used by some people who don't want you to think too hard about the fact that they are putting out technology that is inherently flawed, that they know it, and are more interested in profits than the integrity of information. A lie is an intentionally false statement. I have to believe Google knows its AI Overview makes false statements, yet they put it out there intentionally. Hallucination, drunk uncle malarkey, or lies? You decide. And by so choosing, exert influence.

I'm going to leave you to extrapolate to other important situations where you or someone you trust uses an unreliable intermediary like AI Overview. School, health, work, personal finance. A single screwy web search may seem harmless until you multiply eight and a half billion searches per day by this demonstrated potential to be both inconsistent and wrong. Is this OK?

Let's be the windshield, not the bug, and—to mix a metaphor but keep it automobile-related—put ourselves in the driver's seat. What's your first principle for truth? When do facts matter to you? What's your threshold for trusting an intermediary? When does it matter if you believe your drunk uncle or not? Start by deliberately picking and choosing when you take information at face value when it comes to you via AI. Are the stakes low or high for whether the information is true? Would you go with what your drunk uncle tells you or ignore him? Be a skeptic at whatever level is right for you in that situation. When objective truth matters, AI should be considered wrong until proven right, at least as it's being rolled out to us in the mid-2020s. If you're going to trust AI, consider verifying through a third party that the AI has controls in place to detect and remove misinformation.

Fake text, audio, and video are easily generated with AI. A one-time spike in downloads of my podcast originated in a foreign country a few months before I started writing this book. At the time, we'd published thirty-three episodes, with one or two downloads from the same foreign country. I was excited to see an unexpected bump in downloads, but something looked fishy. All thirty-three episodes had been downloaded at once, something that had never happened before. I looked for information using Google, and it turns out the podcast community sees this type of activity regularly, and not just from foreign countries. The accepted explanation is that these bulk downloads are data harvests by AI companies working on voice generation AI. The hard truth is that I am at increased risk of a "deep fake" of my voice because my recordings have been harvested by an unknown entity in a country sometimes viewed as an adversary to my homeland. For that reason, we don't use last names for guests on the show.

Misinformation can be more subtle, too. I have a couple of friends, one young, one… not so young, who are single and trying to meet people to date. Instagram shows them both a steady stream of content along the lines of "You don't need anyone! You're strong, independent, and don't need anybody!" TikTok feeds another friend a steady stream of "The opposite sex is controlling and mean!" Major social media apps show us what they think will grab and keep our attention. In the olden days of the web, when I worked at Ask Jeeves, we talked about "engagement" and "stickiness" of a website. Could we gain "eyeballs" and keep them looking at a website longer so we could show an ad or sell something? Social media makes billions on the same principle. Behind the scenes of Meta, the understandable set of rules that Instagram and Facebook started with (my friend is interested in boats, so maybe I will be, too) has been replaced entirely by AI. And that AI will do whatever it takes to gain and hold our attention. It learns that negative stereotypes and "us vs them" division will grab lots of people. We're evolutionarily hardwired to respond more to differences than similarities. So that's what social media AI feeds us.

When it comes to truth, social media AI is effectively unmanageable. It may be politically expedient for the leadership of social media companies to say they are increasing or pulling back on their fact-checking efforts, depending on which party is in power. But the reality is they've lost control and couldn't do the fact-checking if they wanted to. The machines they taught to gain and hold our attention move too fast and are too complex to govern. How have you seen misinformation spread in your life? Where could AI have played a role? Did you contribute to the spread? Remember, you teach the machines.

What's the windshield stance with more subtle misinformation? Decide what your first principles are. When do you care that you're being manipulated to gain your attention? Turn awareness into action and make more deliberate choices about what social media you use and how you interpret and consume social media content. Run an experiment: Click on a series of negative or divisive suggestions from the AI. Search for a divisive or negative topic. Observe how your feed changes. Do your friends and loved ones use social media? Have a conversation with them about what you discovered in your experiment. Don't like what you see? Engage with social media AI on your own terms. Vote with your feet and seek alternatives.

2. *Job Loss: Automation over Augmentation?*

Dr. Hinton's next fear is job loss. Artificial intelligence machines can be taught to do work that once only humans could do. A friend asked me for help understanding AI. He was in a new job and had been tasked with learning the alphabet soup of AI: LLM, GPT, GPU, NLP, GenAI. I happily obliged over lunch. We had a great discussion, during which he shared public information about his company's products. One of the products is an AI that watches video feeds from multiple hospital rooms. Its job is to watch the patient on the video and automatically alert a single human mental health monitor (babysitter) to bad stuff—bad stuff like patients trying to harm themselves. The promise was a reduction in the number of humans required to care for at-risk patients. Buy this AI, save even more money because you won't have to pay as many people. On one hand, I am all about reducing the cost and improving outcomes of mental health care so maybe we can have more of it. I've also been in one of those rooms. I've experienced the healing power of human connection and warmth a mental health monitor provides while keeping the patient safe. The business could have sold this new technology as a way to help existing mental health monitors do an even better job, get an even better outcome. Collaborate with mental health monitors to come up with ways to augment their care. Maybe by giving them insight into hidden signals in the patient's behavior and mental state so they can intervene and provide the right support before a crisis occurs. Instead, the business was making the case for saving money by automating work required by regulators and accepting the loss of human connection. Pure automation over augmentation.

We've been here before, just not for knowledge work. The summer I turned nineteen, I earned money as a brick-making machine operator in a factory that made specialty bricks used in high-temperature smelters and kilns. I would press a big red start button and step to the end of a conveyor belt. The brick machine stamped out three bricks and deposited them on the belt every few minutes of my eight- to twelve-hour swing shift, minus two fifteen-minute breaks and thirty minutes for lunch. The raw bricks were fragile and crumbly, made of an exotic (for bricks) mix of specialty clays and minerals. I picked up each brick with very flat hands pressing evenly on two sides of the brick, and deposited it on a metal rack whisked away to an oven by forklift when full. I was probably one of the last summer workers to be hired because the first robotic brick handler was installed that summer. The ten or so full-time operators were offered training as robot technicians. One, a man named Baker, took the opportunity that summer. The other nine refused with reasons varying from "It'll never work for all the types of brick" to "I'm no geek; Baker, you're a nerd!" I left at the end of August to go back to school, never to return. If the company is still in business, my guess is it's with all its brick machines operated by robots, no manual operators in sight.

A few years after I worked at the brick factory, my first job in technology was to get data out of databases. I learned to write code in "Structured Query Language" to select rows and columns from different parts of the database. The language was and remains a well-standardized and powerful way to tell a database what you want (the "query"). The trick was knowing both the language and what the data meant. I understood biology, so was able to quickly and accurately retrieve the right data from a database full of complex biological information. I earned a good living with these skills and others as I built a career solving problems with data and technology. In the two years leading up to writing this book, I saw the same dynamic from the brick factory play out in my technology career. One person in ten embraced new AI tools that "understood" both the structured query language and the meaning of rows and columns in a database. The remaining nine were some combination of frightened, comfortable, and skeptical. My job was to drive adoption of these AI tools because they would allow more scientists to work directly with the data they needed to do critical research in child health. This would scale up and speed up science previously bottlenecked by the relatively small (vs. the needed) number of technical experts who had for decades been the only intermediaries between scientists and databases.

Resistance came from both camps—the technical experts and the scientists. Both would have to step out of their comfort zones. The technical experts would need to give up some autonomy and replace soon-to-be-obsolete skills with new, more advanced knowledge. The scientists would need to learn to use the new AI tools rather than rely on an expert.

It is very human to be uncomfortable with and resist change, but the resistance was discouraging nonetheless, given what was at stake: increased pace and breadth of discovery in child health. I got a grant to create new training programs, but outside of early adopters, the central tendency was to stick with the old model. I am not without empathy. It's hard to learn new skills, especially when you're already working full-time, have kids, and a life outside of work. But just as automation changed manufacturing work, AI is changing knowledge work. Windshield or bug?

Do you remember Louis Winthorpe III and Billy Ray Valentine? Both are fictional characters in the movie *Trading Places*, a 1983 comedy about wealth disparity. Winthorpe, played by Dan Aykroyd, was a privileged genius at making money trading frozen concentrated orange juice, bacon, and other commodities. Valentine, played by Eddie Murphy, was a smart-mouthed hustler living on the streets of Philadelphia. I won't spoil the plot, just share that it's a great window into the 1980s in lots of ways. If you've never seen it, or it's been a while, watch and throw the AI that recommends movies in your streaming service for a loop. As you watch, ponder which characters would have the same job in the age of AI, and which would be out or in a drastically changed job. Hint, Winthorpe wouldn't make it if he held tight to his colorful blazer and open outcry trading on a chaotic market floor covered in slips of paper. He probably wouldn't make it even if he made the transition to electronic trading at a desk somewhere far away from the old stock market exchanges with their bells and hand signals.

The frozen concentrated orange juice and bacon commodities markets are where buyers and sellers bet on the price of breakfast next month or six months from now. Sellers auction off the right to buy their orange crop or hog herd at some future date. This allows farmers to hedge—insure—against the risk of crop failure. Buyers bid to buy the future crop, betting they'll be able to resell juice and bacon for a premium when it's actually time to put breakfast on the table. The auction used to be run by people yelling out, "Who'll give me three hundred dollars a ton for two hundred tons of orange juice for December delivery?" "I'll give you two-eighty a ton!" "I'll give you two-ninety!" "Sold for two-ninety!" Today, the auction happens at nearly light speed between computer programs taught to get the best deal on either side of the trade. This automation also reduces the *transaction* cost to nearly zero, which benefits both buyer and seller. Winthorpe would be on the street running cons with

Valentine. Of course, Winthorpe is a caricature. Humans adapt, including financial traders.

I have a friend, Gerry, who is one of the smartest people I know. They are the first person I know to have their knowledge work completely automated. (Don't worry, the story has a happy ending.) Gerry's career as a trader started in open cry on the floor of the Chicago Board of Trade, transitioned to electronic trading at a desk upstairs, and was ultimately replaced by AI.

I remember one phone call where they asked me, "Hey, how do you speed up a computer network? The algorithm is making money; now we need it to make money faster!"

Gerry's work had evolved from making trades directly based on knowledge of risk and return in the market to using their knowledge to help computer scientists build automated systems. They taught the machine to make more money with less risk than they could manually. This got boring, so after twenty-five years, Gerry transitioned to a new career in high-end building renovation and construction. Lots of other traders had to make the shift much earlier, like our intransigent fictional Winthorpe. They were "old school" traders who didn't want to or couldn't contribute to the automation of their jobs like Gerry did.

It's no surprise that some of the biggest Big AI users directly focus their data and AI efforts on only two areas of the economy: finance and healthcare. AI in other areas are left to partners, startups, and other big companies already working in the area, like Monsanto in agriculture. Financial services (including insurance) represent more than $7 trillion, healthcare $18 trillion in the U.S. alone. Finance and healthcare are also almost entirely based on expert humans performing knowledge work.

The same Big AI companies investing hundreds of billions of dollars choose to dig into the two areas of the economy with the most valuable (in dollars) knowledge work. Don't get me wrong. They've set it up so they'll get a piece of everything. Startups and big companies in law, publishing, advertising, engineering, software development, and entertainment incorporate Big AI foundation models into their own products and pay a toll to Big AI. But healthcare and finance are where Big AI is focused "in-house." Finance and healthcare are where they're looking for "partners" to "co-invest" in data aggregation and training AI. You better believe each company intends to win the race to develop powerful and lucrative foundation models specific to healthcare and finance. The prize is the biggest possible share in potentially trillions of dollars transferred from human worker payrolls to Big AI service fees.

My friend Gerry lived through the leading edge of this inevitable trend. As their knowledge of the commodities market and work as a trader became less valuable, they adapted and taught the machine to analyze risk and return and make trades. Gerry moved on, finding creative new trading opportunities, figuring out how to make money, and then taught the machine the new stuff. And on and on until it was more interesting to move to a completely different field.

People who do work based on knowledge and cognition watched automation drastically change the economic prospects of their fellow citizens who worked in what little domestic manufacturing remained in the U.S. Large corporations grew wealthy or just remained in business through robotic automation of what they couldn't move to lower-wage economies. The same is happening and will happen to knowledge workers. Call the bank customer service number to combine the balance of two accounts and close one. Twenty years ago, you talked to someone in Texas or Minnesota. Ten years ago, you interacted with someone in Mumbai, India. Now you interact with AI that is rapidly improving its ability to solve your problem. If the AI can't help you, that failure is recorded and you're directed to a person in a low-wage or low-regulation economy. The audio of your interaction with that person and the resulting actions they take to deal with your accounts are recorded and used to teach the machine to solve the new problem. That is, unless you have a lot of money on deposit in the bank; then you may speak with a real person in Texas. For now.

The best software engineers I known in my career live by the mantra, "My job is to put myself out of a job." Here is a real story from the stress-detection project I expand on later in the chapter: The job is to retrieve heart rate data from two watches and combine it into one dataset where the data from one watch can be compared to the data from the other. The best engineer will write the most efficient, powerful, and user-friendly software possible so they never have to solve this same problem again. New watch? Someone else can adjust a couple of settings and it's done. Other, lesser software engineers might write unique code for each watch, code that requires them to fiddle and be in the loop. With the advent of AI, the best software engineers I know are immediately figuring out how the AI can write code for them so they can move on to solve harder, more important problems. They'll continue to do this, just like Gerry did with trading.

If you're a knowledge worker, the value of your current work is going to change. Do you read, summarize, and write reports? Do you write or edit words? Do you write or test code? Do you provide financial advice? Do you analyze data repeatedly? Do you research and make recommendations? Do you answer the phone and help people? Do you teach? Do you decide where to invest money? Do you make podcasts? Do you interpret lab results and make a diagnosis? Do you act? Do you edit video? Do you read x-rays and identify bone fractures or other problems? Do you design interior or exterior spaces? Do you talk to people about their cognitive and behavioral problems on the phone or video? Do you compose or perform music? Value real estate? Design bridges? At least the routine aspects of your work will be performed better, faster, or more cheaply by a machine. There is too much money to be saved or made for it not to happen, at least in the U.S. You will have to adapt or see your income go down. Use AI in your work in any way and you are already adapting. Windshield or bug?

You choose windshield! What to do?

Start by reflecting on work you do repeatedly but with your brain instead of your hands. We're used to thinking of repetitive labor as something that happens on an assembly line. Repetitive physical labor is subject to automation by physical machines with moving parts. Repetitive *cognitive* labor is subject to automation by AI machines with cognitive parts.

Before getting to knowledge work, consider how AI will change the time-is-money business of artists and skilled craftspeople. If you're an artist, a sculptor, a furniture-maker, a metalworker, a stonemason, a gardener, a chef, or a pipe fitter you need to use AI and AI-enabled software to work smarter, not harder. Artificial intelligence running on your smartphone can collect and analyze data about your work to help you make more money from your time. Artificial intelligence–enabled purchasing services can help you find the best deals on materials. Artificial intelligence can help you write your own advertising copy and generate your own graphics. Many of the business services you depend on, or wish you could tap into, may become cheaper because of AI. At the same time, be prepared for your customers who don't work with their hands to go through economic upheaval.

Most important? Do. Not. Give. Away. Your. Data. I cannot emphasize enough the degree to which the current U.S. corporate economy is harvesting the data of workers so that it can put them out of a job at some point in the future. This is not because these corporations are somehow evil. It's because they are intrinsically and legally obligated to survive and thrive using new technology to increase productivity. And productivity is calculated as output per worker: dollars of revenue or profit divided by number of workers. In an ideal world, the whole pie will grow fast enough that every worker will continue to be employed and maybe even see their income grow faster than inflation. This happened for the most part during the bottom-up phase of the first Industrial Revolution. The AI-driven industrial revolution of the knowledge economy is *starting* with top-down industrialization, as we've discussed. Increased productivity through automating the work of expensive analysts, billing experts, doctors, lawyers, engineers, nurses, accountants, and home health workers is the model for success I see gaining traction with the people who sign the checks when AI vendors come calling in my professional life, at least in the U.S. Cost reduction is the first stop for entrenched organizations that have difficulty innovating. We've already offshored or automated just about everything else possible, so knowledge work comes next. So what leverage do you and I have? The data we generate in the course of our work. Consider yourself an independent contractor, the expertise you've gained over a career to be your intellectual property. The data you generate can be used to teach a machine what you know and how to do your work. Your employment contract almost certainly says that your employer owns this data. They do unless you speak up about it. Are you a lawyer? Ask the partners in your firm how they plan to compensate you for the use of your briefs, memos, and contracts to train AI. Are you a doctor, nurse, or billing agent? Ask your practice or hospital administrators how they plan to cut you in on the savings they hope to achieve through using your notes, diagnoses, reports, and discharge summaries to automate aspects of your work. Are you an investment advisor? Ask your managers how they plan on making you whole from the use of your client communications over the phone or via email to automate aspects of your relationship-building. Ask your leadership if their corporate contract with Big AI allows those companies to use your documents, emails, or code to teach AI about your industry, company, or specific job. If the answer is yes, then ask how much money they saved on the contract by agreeing to those terms. Suggest that perhaps they could share that with you and your fellow workers. If you're an author, carefully read the terms of the self-publishing service you use to put out your first book to figure out if your writing will be used to teach a machine to write books about AI.

Sound radical? The concept of a "data collective" is emerging among economists as a potential counterbalance to even out the economic risks posed by AI. In theory, fair distribution of economic gains that are only possible through the use of human data to train AI would grow the whole pie. Allow us all to share in the profits from this amazing new technology. It's not just theoretical. In 2025, the concept is just starting to be tested via the first lawsuits against

Big AI companies for copyright infringement. Turns out if you're a publisher or a clothing designer (Gerkin, 2023; Rogelberg, 2024), you may think it's economically unfair when your text and pictures are harvested, potentially without your knowledge, incorporated into a foundation model, and then monetized by a Big AI company so people can write books and design clothes derived from your work. The question is, if the *New York Times* wins its suit against OpenAI, will it distribute a portion of the proceeds to its journalists, copywriters, and editors? Maybe. Maybe not. Ironically, twenty-five years ago, as the *defendant* in another lawsuit, the *New York Times* argued against its current position versus OpenAI (Pope, 2024). At that time, the U.S. Supreme Court decided against the *Times* and in favor of a group of freelance journalists whose articles the *Times* had sold piecemeal to database companies without permission (Supreme Court of the United States, 2001). We've been here before. You teach the machines.

Other economies may attempt to manage their AI industrialization following the example of Japan's Meiji Restoration in the late 1800s. The new leadership of Japan actively managed the transfer of industrial technology into Japan to maximize benefit and minimize harm. Keep an eye on countries that deliberately manage the AI Industrial Revolution so as to at least try to benefit all. In the U.S., and by extension many of the places where Big AI companies dominate, it's a free-for-all driven by a few corporations with lots of political influence.

As I write this, my three children are just about to graduate from college, in college, and just about to enter college. All of them are entering an era of change. Guidance I (try to) give them? I start with my own first principles. Be nice. Get stuff done. Make things less crappy. When it comes to AI, I try to help them see that it will bring change. Stick to first principles when the ground shifts under you. Embrace the change and you'll be just fine. I emphasize to them the importance of two things: They need to use AI, and they need to learn about a specific area of the world they're interested in, one that is constantly changing, the faster the better.

To succeed in an AI world, you have to be good at augmenting your work and your life with AI so that you can invest your time in what AI can't do (yet). Use AI so you know what's possible. Use it consistently so you know when it can do something new and useful, when it gets something wrong, or when it gets something right it previously got wrong. Use AI so you're not competing with it to do work that can be automated. Dream up and experiment with creative uses of AI nobody else thought of. Be the person who figures out how to use AI and help your family, friends, coworkers, and employer adopt and adapt. Use AI to pursue interests previously out of reach.

Regarding interests, I try to guide my kids to constantly learn about something they find intriguing. Their current interests are biology, art, and creating value in a business, respectively. The more they know about their interests, the more they can tell when AI gets things right and when it gets them wrong. The more they know about the world outside the bubble of AI, the more they understand AI isn't perfect and they can be informed and critical consumers.

Regarding change, I try to guide them to be more than comfortable with change. I say they must excel at finding opportunity and value in disruption and changing circumstances. Because things are going to change a lot faster over the next couple of decades vs the last couple.

I also encourage my kids, and you, to learn to do things with your hands. To be creative. My kids probably don't think I'm serious, but I made a standing offer to pay for them to learn a trade in addition to their higher education—welding, carpentry, plumbing, electrical wiring, house painting, stone masonry, tilework. Makeup artistry, hair styling. Avalanche control, emergency medical response.

Knowing how to use AI and do valuable work with their hands means they have a killer combination. Combine AI, hands-on work, and creativity and you're futureproof. Pure knowledge work is likely to pay relatively less on average in the medium term. If the AI Industrial Revolution plays out on the more pessimistic track, wealth will continue to concentrate, but wealthy people still clog their toilets, want new kitchens, and value artistry.

Want a good outcome? Use AI. Learn constantly. Pursue change. Don't give away your data.

3. *Killer Robots*

You're not going to hear much about the use of AI in weapons of war. The *Terminator* movie franchise made robots with guns into a public relations nightmare for the AI industry. That doesn't mean it isn't happening. Geoffrey Hinton called this out as one of his reasons for resigning from Google. This could mean he knows something of what might be happening behind a top-secret curtain. Before we get to AI actually blowing people up, it's important to consider that not all conflict involves the guns and missiles of a "hot war."

In my professional life I have encountered credible hacking threats and actual attacks on critical health infrastructure. I've briefed three-letter agencies, not on defense against, but, scarily, the *detection* of theft of what I consider to be some of the most sensitive human information in existence. That means I was asked to come up with ways to figure out if information had been stolen *after* the unseen and undetected theft took place by a state-sponsored attacker.

Cyberattacks, hacking, ransomware. Whatever you call it, state sponsored attacks on people's digital lives have grown into a new Cold War. Real examples of attacks include tricking you or me into giving access to our bank account, encrypting a hospital's patient data so it can't be used then extorting ransom for the decoder key, planting misinformation about a political candidate in social media, causing power outages, and remotely destroying nuclear weapons manufacturing equipment. "State sponsored" means that a government or agency in a government looks the other way, pays for, staffs, or even directly carries out attacks. Up to a certain point in political conflict, "good guy" and "bad guy" depend on your point of view. When it comes to cyberattacks, everyone does it. Artificial intelligence lowers the bar for what it takes to fight in this new, digital Cold War. You don't have a bunch of sophisticated hackers to write malicious computer code? Use AI to write the code instead. A hard-liner is up for election in a rival country? Use freely available AI to generate and post fake video of the candidate doing something sketchy in a hotel room. An economic competitor is moving in on an emerging market you want for yourself? Use AI to manipulate the local stock market with automatic trades. AI scales up information warfare. Flyers dropped from airplanes, propaganda broadcasts over the radio, and even "troll farms" are being replaced by AI trained to push issues through social media, finance, education, anywhere people interact with a stream of information.

Military AI emerges somewhere between information warfare and shooting warfare. The military uses, or will use, AI for lots of the same purposes for which it's being utilized in other areas. Logistics, intelligence gathering, management. The primary concern, however, is a category of military AI known as Lethal Autonomous Weapons Systems (LAWS). To the layperson, a weapons system is lethal and autonomous when a machine picks a target and fires a gun or missile without a human in the loop. Policy and military experts, not surprisingly, have to wrestle with a gray area. In 2025, the United Nations is an intermediary for governments to try to agree on a definition of autonomous weapons systems.

They publish helpful information useful for thinking about AI in general, not just for weapons:

> *Autonomous weapons systems require "autonomy" to perform their functions in the absence of direction or input from a human actor. Artificial intelligence is not a prerequisite for the functioning of autonomous weapons systems, but, when incorporated, AI could further enable such systems. In other words, not all autonomous weapons systems incorporate AI to execute particular tasks. Autonomous capabilities can be provided through pre-defined tasks or sequences of actions based on specific parameters, or through using artificial intelligence tools to derive behavior from data, thus allowing the system to make independent decisions or adjust behavior based on changing circumstances. Artificial intelligence can also be used in an assistance role in systems that are directly operated by a human. For example, a computer vision system operated by a human could employ artificial intelligence to identify and draw attention to notable objects in the field of vision, without having the capacity to respond to those objects autonomously in any way. (United Nations Office for Disarmament Affairs, 2023)*

There's some particularly helpful wording in the above paragraph: "…using artificial intelligence tools to derive behavior from data, thus allowing the system to make independent decisions or adjust behavior based on changing circumstances." Rewritten in a more human context, we get: "using your eyes and ears (data) to figure out how to behave (derive behavior), allowing you to make your own decisions or adjust what you do based on changes in the world around you (changing circumstances)." Truly autonomous driving lines up nicely with this definition. AI driving a car in a safety-critical situation with potential injury or death from a traffic accident if the AI decides to accelerate or brake at the wrong time. When a weapon meets the same definition, AI makes another kind of life-and-death decision.

People often have an intuitive, negative reaction to drone warfare. A missile fired from a drone piloted by a flight officer hundreds or thousands of miles away can be viewed as wrong relative to a missile fired from an airplane by its pilot in the cockpit. The invasion of Ukraine by Russia took modern drone warfare to a whole other level from its origins in post-911 conflict. Suddenly, hundreds of thousands of drones were deployed—at first to drop grenades from above on nearby enemy positions and vehicles, then for one-way flights of explosives directly into the same targets, destroying the drone in the process. Both Russia and Ukraine used drones, but Ukraine, with its smaller population, leaned on the technology more. A soldier is safer piloting an explosive drone into a bunker from a few hundred yards away than fighting their way across an open battlefield to deliver the same explosives. Ukraine also embraced the "first-person view" (FPV) drone early in the conflict. A soldier wears goggles that display the view from a camera on the front of the drone. They "see" what's in front of the drone through the goggles as if they were right there. The soldier uses a hand-held remote control with joysticks and buttons to pilot the explosive-laden drone into the tank, bunker, or concentration of enemy soldiers. This visual immersion of the goggles enables the soldier to make more precise and rapid flight maneuvers than if they are looking at a screen. In fact, the FPV drone gained its first popularity in drone racing a decade earlier. A second, larger observation drone is used to view the attack from above and look for the next targets for a stream of one-way explosive drones to hit. Recordings of FPV drone attacks are regularly posted to social media.

What does this all have to do with global geopolitical concerns about military AI? Why did United Nations leaders suddenly gain traction on the issue in 2023, after first raising it in reports to the Human Rights Council ten years earlier? What does any of this have to do with Geoffrey Hinton calling out autonomous weapons systems when he resigned from Google in 2023?

In the U.S., we can look backward at an intertwined cast of characters starting in the first Obama administration and continuing through multiple administrations of both parties. Our players are

Eric Schmidt, Robert Work, and Peter Thiel—all patriots and, I believe, acting in good faith, though one could argue in apparent if not actual conflict of interest. The following may be hard to follow because the natural revolving door between government, the military, and industry is hard to follow:

- Eric Schmidt, then-CEO of Google, was appointed by President Obama in 2009 to the President's Council of Advisors on Science and Technology.
- Along with others, under Eric Schmidt's leadership, Google funded (and continues to fund) the Center for a New American Security.
- Robert Work, retired Marine Colonel, was appointed Undersecretary of the Navy in 2013, leaving soon after to run the Center for New American Security for about a year until appointed Deputy Secretary of Defense in 2014.
- During his tenure at the Center for a New American Security, Robert Work advocated that the U.S. address the long-term threat of adversaries gaining an advantage in military AI.
- Peter Thiel, a longtime technology executive and investor, co-founded Palantir Technologies in 2003 to develop security software and now military AI. After the 2008 financial crisis, the first Obama administration paid Palantir for software used to detect fraud in stimulus funding and Medicare payments.
- Throughout both Obama administrations, Eric Schmidt maintained a professional relationship with Peter Thiel, with the two

appearing on multiple technology panels together.

- During Robert Work's tenure in the Obama administration and subsequent first Trump administration, Google received a contract to develop military AI for the Pentagon. After employee protests, Google transferred the contract to Palantir in 2019.
- Eric Schmidt continued as chairman and then technical advisor to Google's parent company, Alphabet, until 2020.
- From 2019 to 2021, Eric Schmidt and Robert Work co-chaired the bipartisan National Security Commission on AI, which advocated for investment in AI for national security.
- In 2021, Eric Schmidt funded and founded the Strategic Competitive Studies Project, which has Robert Work on its Board of Directors.
- In 2022, Google and Palantir announced a strategic partnership.
- In 2022, Eric Schmidt and Peter Thiel launched America's Frontier Fund, an investment fund focused on national security in microchip manufacture critical to AI, weapons, and the economy. Their new investment organization lobbied the government for one billion in funding and won a lead role in an international investment fund led by the former CEO of the Central Intelligence Agency's venture capital subsidiary, In-Q-Tel. Official Pentagon policy and Palantir's publicly stated goal is that military AI augments human decision making. Palantir continued to win defense contracts from the U.S. and other governments throughout the first half of the

2020s.

I lay out these circumstantial points to illustrate that the historical relationship between the technology industry and national security apparatus is alive and well in the age of AI. I also lay out these circumstances to prepare you for a theory I'll get to shortly.

The revolving door is a good thing if you take seriously the national security threat posed by hostile use of AI (which I do). It also presents by its nature potential conflicts of interest and the need for transparency to stakeholders like you and me. Stakeholders who also have a responsibility to educate ourselves and participate, not just sit back and throw around conspiracy theories like your drunk uncle. In their final report to the National Security Commission on AI before it was dissolved in 2021, Chairman Schmidt and Vice-Chairman Work stated, "Americans have not yet seriously grappled with how profoundly the AI revolution will impact society, the economy, and national security." They were and unfortunately continue to be right. It's a scary world out there.

Russia stated in 2020 that it intended to replace soldiers with lethal autonomous weapons systems. Russia has established a drone weapons program in China, resulting in the U.S. placing sanctions on Chinese entities. Simultaneously, the Ukrainian military's success rate for drone attacks reportedly rose from fifty percent before 2023 to more than eighty percent in 2024, reportedly in large part through use of drones running Palantir software. Turns out killer robots weren't so sci-fi after all.

From a purely professional technical standpoint, I consider the video of drone attacks coming out of the Russian invasion of Ukraine to be priceless for training AI. The repeated nature of the attacks under varying landscape, foliage, weather, and countermeasures provides a rich sample of real-world images for teaching machines to identify targets. Surveillance drones' simultaneous recording of attack drone strikes provides built-in labeling of the result—hit or miss. The recording of front-line soldiers' commands and flight telemetry over and over during actual combat drone maneuvers paired with video and geospatial location under varying conditions provides a near-ideal, unique data set for teaching machines to fly drones into targets.

Russia also uses FPV attack and surveillance drones and is in a position to collect the same unique data and share it with its allies, or at least with "the enemy of my enemy is my friend."

As I mentioned a few paragraphs ago, I'm going to advance an informed theory that attempts to explain this landscape. Because of the top-secret, or at least highly confidential, nature of the situation, my theory is certain to be a simplification of complex events.

The theory: Eric Schmidt followed in the footsteps of patriotic industrialists before him. He and others identified the risk that adversaries would develop military AI that could defeat the U.S. and its allies in the future. "They" would have more or better killer robots than the U.S. "They" would have more or better AI-enabled cyberweapons. Because he is simultaneously a patriot and a capitalist, Schmidt aligned Google with the Pentagon to drive research and development through multiple presidential administrations. Simultaneously, Peter Thiel aligned Palantir with the Pentagon and other U.S. government agencies to develop AI for national security, also through multiple presidential administrations. When Google's employees forced a change because of ideological disagreement over the company's involvement in military AI, Eric Schmidt and Peter Thiel worked together at the top of their companies to successfully transition the project from Google to Palantir. Schmidt and his original national security partner, Robert Work, continued to build the case for U.S. investments in military AI. Palantir developed its business through contracts with Israel and other U.S. allies, in addition to the U.S. A goldmine of unique training data became available from drone warfare in Ukraine. The U.S. directly and indirectly facilitated systematic and large-scale acquisition by Palantir of drone warfare data from Ukraine. Palantir used this data to rapidly accelerate development of military AI for drone warfare. Palantir simultaneously contracted directly with the Ukrainian government and military to develop and field systems that enable front-line soldiers to continue to train and fine-tune the performance of its military AI. United States intelligence agencies obtained evidence that Russia had been sharing drone warfare video data with China in return for access to Chinese drones equipped with military AI.

Now, in a lethal feedback loop, China also gets data from front-line Russian soldiers on the performance of its AI. The U.S. and China cannot take the risk that the other develops lethal autonomous weapons systems, so a secret military AI arms race is under way. Palantir, as a private company, is able to research and develop lethal autonomous AI, and the hundreds of billions of dollars in unrestricted aid going to Ukraine can be used to pay for it. United Nations policy makers receive reports of the pursuit of lethal autonomous AI by both the U.S. and China. On the U.S. side, the AI arms race, at least in part, involves Google through its partnership with Palantir, and almost certainly other Big AI companies as well. The United Nations starts to develop and advocate for policy to reduce harm of military AI. I'm an outsider so this is just a theory. It is also my theory that Geoffrey Hinton knows enough from his insider status that he decides to resign.

As a child of the 1980s, I lived with the reality of nuclear deterrence through mutually assured destruction. Ten years before I was born, the U.S. and Russia came to the brink of nuclear war during the Cuban missile crisis, itself a response to perceived escalation by the U.S. placing weapons closer to the Soviet Union. We, as global citizens, eventually de-escalated through reciprocal nuclear arms control and non-proliferation treaties. We're not there with military AI. We don't yet (and hopefully never will) have the equivalent horrific example of the use of nuclear weapons in the bombing of Hiroshima and Nagasaki at the end of World War II, followed by decades of living under the real fear of nuclear holocaust. However, state or state-sponsored actors have deployed AI in cyberattacks. Russia has targeted civilians with drones in isolated terror attacks. It is a matter of scale to get to swarms of cheap, fully autonomous lethal drones overwhelming military defenses or, worse, being used in a terror attack on a stadium full of people. Possibly worse yet, bad people could use powerful AI to degrade or destroy military and civilian digital infrastructure. Or use AI-generated misinformation to destroy trust in our institutions and fellow citizens. This is the through line Geoffrey Hinton, many other technology leaders, and the United Nations are concerned about.

What can you do? I suggest buying a cup of coffee or something stronger for the Chief Information Security Officer or equivalent at your company; they're dealing with more than you can imagine. After that, get informed and come to your own conclusion on whether or how military AI in any of its forms are acceptable. It is certainly inevitable. You may go on to demand more transparency about military AI programs, or at least how the money flows in what is an evolution of the Cold War military-industrial complex. You may advocate politically against an AI arms race, in favor of mutual defense agreements, or for spending on offensive and defensive capabilities. You may talk to your peers and kids about the importance of cybersecurity and data protection. You may work toward a global ban on military AI. You may choose a career developing effective AI weapons. It's up to you. You teach the machines.

4. "Other"

Geoffrey Hinton may also be concerned with other side effects and pitfalls. A few of the more fundamental ones follow.

Bias

Artificial intelligence is as biased as the data and people who teach it. The machine will learn from the people who tell it what it gets correct when looking at its training data. If that data reflects unfair biases because it contains only a biased view of the world, then the AI will have those biases. If the people teaching the machine hold a biased view of what's correct and that makes it through to the machine during training, then the AI will have those biases.

Imagine you take videos of cats. Like, a weirdly large number of cat videos. Say two thousand and counting. You prefer orange tabby and black cats, especially when they're sleeping (so cute!). Your two-thousand videos contain mostly sleeping orange and black cats, with the rest showing brown, gray, and spotted cats mostly not sleeping—play fighting with each other, chasing birds, and eating. Your videos are in a cloud service hosted by a Big AI company. The same Big AI company also sells a home-smart speaker device recently upgraded with a camera.

Pat, a bright young marketing person, pitches a new feature for their camera devices: "Bad Kitty: your AI cat babysitter!" Even better, Pat gets Nick Bruel, author of the beloved *Bad Kitty* children's books on board to co-brand the thing. Pat's vice president loves it and greenlights the project. Since it's legal, you've accepted the terms of use, and live in the U.S., the Big AI company gives your cat pictures to the AI team without asking or informing you. The team sends your pictures overseas for labeling by low-wage AI workers, again without asking or informing you. The workers dutifully tag the videos of sleeping orange and black cats with "good." They tag the videos of mischievous brown, gray, and spotted cats with "bad." Pat's VP is in a hurry to publicly announce the product at the company's rapidly approaching sparkly launch event in Las Vegas, so the AI team quickly teaches a machine to automatically recognize cats misbehaving on camera and yell "NO! BAD KITTY!" through the speaker. Just before the Vegas event, Nick Bruel pulls out of the deal. Turns out he has an orange cat that is a complete jerk and an angel of a brown cat. The pre-release camera speaker he got in the mail gives his orange cat a pass when it knocks the toothpaste cap down the drain and yells nonstop at his poor brown cat. The VP is embarrassed, fires Pat, and cats everywhere breathe a sigh of relief because they don't have to live in a surveillance state.

A silly make-believe example, but an entirely realistic illustration of how harmful bias can make its way into AI out in the world. Look for articles about bias in AI and you'll find plenty of examples in much more critical areas of our lives. I encountered a near-miss formative example early on in my work.

In a research study I did together with a behavioral health scientist, we wanted to figure out how to help caregivers and teachers by detecting stress in nonverbal children who couldn't otherwise say, "Hey! I'm freaking out over here!" We taught AI to recognize stress from changes in heart rate detected by commercially available heart-rate watches. We had an intern with brown skin working on the otherwise all-white research team. She figured out that one of the otherwise ideal brands of watch gave bad readings on her skin but not on white skin. We immediately excluded the watch, recruited study participants with different skin tones, thanked the science gods for the luck of that intern, and kicked ourselves for not thinking about what could happen if we hadn't had her. The research continues, the AI has promise, but it could have started out with a very damaging implicit bias against people with brown skin.

Wondering how we taught the machine to recognize stress without doing harm to vulnerable nonverbal children? We collected a bag of tricks, including a remote-control rubber rat that darted across the floor, a puzzle that couldn't be solved, a jack-in-the-box with a scary clown face and spooky music, and a wind-up jumping rubber spider. Research participants, first adults, then children with their parents, were put in a room wearing the heart-rate watch and subjected to jump scares. We collected heart-rate data and time-synched video so we could see when changes in heart rate co-occurred with the rat darting across the floor or the creepy jack-in-the-box popping. Not my favorite moment as a researcher, but everyone was informed and consented ahead of time and the work was for a very good cause. Can't make this stuff up.

What can you do about harmful bias in AI? Turn awareness into questions that ultimately drive expectations and accountability. Ask your doctor if they're using AI to help them care for you. If they say yes, ask them how the AI has been taught to avoid harming patients from any one demographic. Pay attention to proposed regulations and legislation to require transparency and mitigation of harmful biases. When your employer rolls out new AI, ask how it was trained to avoid harmful bias. Better yet, ask how it will be monitored for harmful bias going forward. Pessimistically, recognize that AI could be used to deliberately reinforce bias in conjunction with misinformation. Bias toward buying a brand of toothpaste, for example. Bias against voting for one candidate over another. Be on the lookout and question how AI may reinforce your own very human biases to manipulate you. Optimistically, recognize that AI can help reduce bias, too. A teacher who is biased to be more sympathetic to kids with one skin color may tend to ignore signs of distress in kids with a different skin color. Artificial intelligence that can detect stress in kids with skin of any color is a powerful equalizer to get a better outcome for all children.

Electricity

Industrial AI companies need more than the existing electricity grid you depend on to light your home and run your coffee maker. The biggest AI companies are like aluminum producers in that industrial AI needs high-volume, stable electricity. Aluminum smelters are often located right next to big fossil fuel, hydroelectric, or geothermal electricity generators—sometimes built just for that purpose, whether nearby communities wanted them or not. And just as aluminum producers bring in a steady supply of bauxite ore, AI data centers bring in a steady supply of raw data. Aluminum companies bring bauxite to aluminum smelters. Raw data flows into GPU computers. Aluminum smelters need lots of electricity to electrolyze bauxite into primary aluminum billets. Big AI data centers need lots of electricity to train foundation model AI from raw data. Aluminum producers' billets are subsequently turned into cars, soda cans, and fishing boats. Big AI's foundation model AI are subsequently turned into chatbots, x-ray diagnostics, and search assistants.

In 2025, AI companies are already using a lot of electricity from fossil fuels to train AI. They know burning even more coal and natural gas for their rapidly expanding data centers will put a lot of carbon into the atmosphere. They know this will make it harder for them to make money from customers concerned about climate change. They know that what they're doing will add to the risk of floods, hurricanes, droughts—extreme weather affecting the economy they depend on and the data centers full of their AI computers.

Industrial AI is already mitigating this side effect with nuclear energy and its low- to no-carbon output. The pitfall? More nuclear waste in the form of spent fuel. Although fuel reprocessing technologies promise to reduce the final volume of high-level radioactive waste, there will still be more to safely dispose of for the hundreds of years it will take to lose its radioactivity. Consensus favors burial deep underground in stable geological formations without nearby groundwater. Absent these sites of high-level waste will continue to accumulate in "casks" at the reactor site. China, Japan, Canada, and many EU countries are in the process of selecting and designing long-term burial locations. The U.S. has one but, for political reasons, has been unable to license it for use. What can you do? Decide how this reality matches up with your values and make choices accordingly.

Cooling Water

Data centers use water to manage heat. Effectively, all the electricity consumed to train and operate AI is turned into heat. Data goes into the GPU. The GPU burns electricity to do calculations. The process releases heat. The GPU produces data.

Think about when your laptop, phone, or computer gets hot when it works hard. Global estimates for 2025 put annual electricity usage by data centers above five hundred terawatt hours (Masanet et al., 2020), equivalent to two trillion of those red heat lamp bulbs keeping french fries warm. Graphics processing units get slow when they get hot, necessitating quick removal of heat from the data center. This process requires billions and billions and billions of gallons of water, ultimately evaporated to achieve actual cooling (think about pictures of nuclear power plant cooling towers; that's what's going on). The need for data center cooling water comes on top of the need for water to cool the nuclear reactors that generate the electricity in the first place. Usually, this is fresh water because salt water is corrosive and bad for pipes and machinery. This is fresh water that would otherwise stay in the ground, a river, or a lake and be available for fish to swim in and people to drink.

What to do? Same as with electricity. No matter what you think, electricity and cooling water are costs, so companies have an incentive to work to minimize usage. Decide how water usage by AI companies aligns with your values and make decisions accordingly. Make purchasing decisions, or ask your employer or stockbroker to make purchasing decisions, based on your views about water usage by AI companies. The point is that every industry we depend on in our modern lives consumes resources. Artificial intelligence is no different. Just as with packaging, transportation, and housing, your responsibility is to be informed and make decisions about how you consume AI that align with your values.

Individual Rights

Your unique data is likely the most valuable asset held by any technology company you've knowingly given it to, or that has it anyway because you agreed to obscure Terms of Service (at least in the U.S.). Mark Gorenberg and Ash Fontana were two of the first venture capitalists to invest in AI. They wrote an article in 2016 about the new rules for venture capital in technology that includes the following about the new requirement for a start-up to have a data strategy:

> *Data Strategy: A crucial part of your plan to build an intelligent software product. A clean, unique data set is a competitive advantage in itself (so don't sell it!). From there, you can start building predictive models with your customers' data and turning successful experiments into features that help them make decisions. Finally, you will have a product that uses incremental data to improve models; making the product better, attracting more customers, getting more data and so on — a "Virtuous Loop." (Fontana, Ash, & Mark Gorenberg, 2016).*

Use of your data to gain a competitive advantage is a fundamental pillar of AI. Your individual rights to correct, mask, prevent use of, or simply delete that data are in direct opposition to the profit motive of technology companies. At its best, this remains a virtuous cycle where use of your data directly benefits you. There are no guarantees, especially in the U.S.

While traveling abroad in the EU, I checked the privacy policy of a major U.S.-based news website I subscribe to. Since I was accessing the news site from the EU, I found (and have a great screen capture of) a page that stated the news site and ninety-four of its "partners" would store and access any personal data they could collect through the site to do all sorts of things, including "understand audiences through statistics or combinations of data from different sources." I was also able to see the full list of ninety-four partners and the exact use they make of my data. I had the choice of opting in to this arrangement. No sharing would happen if I did nothing or rejected the option. When I got back to the U.S., I went to the privacy policy to find I did not have the same rights to control my data. In place of the relatively clear EU-mandated language, there was a confusing and ultimately opaque set of terms that kind of disclosed what would happen with "partners" unless I was a resident of California, Oregon, or Nevada, in which case I had some other rights. But not at home in Pennsylvania!

The hard reality is that there's a massive global marketplace where your data is collected, used to maximum competitive advantage, sold, traded, and monetized. Friends who work in marketing, politics, and philanthropy have access to scarily detailed subscription-based databases that can be used to profile you and your behavior down to the most minute detail. Up until the mid-2010s, I had to call my bank to file an "international travel plan" when I was travelling abroad so they would allow credit and debit card transactions to go through. Now? The bank has an AI model that's been taught everything about me. It'll allow a late-night poutine purchase in Quebec City to dilute the beer with cheesy gravy fries, no travel plan required!

Banks aren't the only large organizations that know, or are able to know, everything about you recorded in the digital world. PRISM is the code name for a surveillance program run by the U.S. National Security Agency. Under oversight, government agencies are able to search through your and my individual-level data processed by U.S. technology companies, including all the Big AI players.

PRISM is the program brought to light by Edward Snowden in 2013. It continues and is the basis for a series of legal actions brought in the EU by a private nonprofit called None of Your Business (NOYB), a comical name if the issue weren't so serious. The organization was founded by Austrian lawyer Max Schrems who, while studying at Santa Clara University in Silicon Valley, was blown away by Facebook's lack of respect for individual privacy. Schrems used the EU's privacy laws to get his hands on Facebook's store of his own personal data. As a result of his actions, a patchwork collection of oversight was put in place to allow citizens of the EU to safely use Facebook, Apple, Google, Microsoft, etc. The oversight is fragile and was gutted in the early months of the second

Trump administration. It remains to be seen if and how the oversight is reinstated. I encourage you to spend some time reading about the privacy rights action being taken by NOYB on their website: www.noyb.eu.

This all gets creepier when you consider that the companies subject to PRISM collect and can be forced to share pictures, videos, voice recordings of you, your parents, your kids. Not to mention your fingerprints. Travel by air in the U.S. lately? Notice the "optional" face scan going into use at airport security checkpoints?

On a recent flight, the security worker was rapidly and emphatically instructing passengers to insert their state-issued ID and look into the camera to be scanned. The facial recognition scan is technically optional, as stated in the fine print on the sign off to the side, but what I saw did not at all appear to be voluntary. My line didn't have it in place yet; otherwise, I would have refused and had more to share here! The same systems are going into place on some European airlines. China isn't the only surveillance state.

Your individual copyright is also at risk from AI. A copyright gives an author or creator "the exclusive legal right to reproduce, publish, sell, or distribute the matter and form of something (such as a literary, musical, or artistic work)" per Webster's dictionary. Copyright protects you and me from someone taking our writing, music, art, or performance and using it for their own financial gain. Three publishers, including the *New York Times*, have brought a lawsuit before a U.S. federal court, arguing that OpenAI and

Microsoft are making money from copying and processing news articles without asking or paying for the right. The roughly fourteen million authors and editors of Wikipedia articles may also have a complaint, as their work was copied and used to train OpenAI's ChatGPT, among other AI. What if the corporations had to pay all the authors of Wikipedia a toll for redistributing their knowledge?

There are more known side effects and pitfalls you could inform yourself about. By all means, go dig in and be more informed. But AI, in the U.S. especially, is happening whether you like it or not. Your job is to maximize benefit and minimize harm according to your first principles. There are many unknown side effects and pitfalls ahead. You must accept uncertainty and be prepared to respond to events as they unfold. You teach the machines.

Knowledge, Uncertainty, and Ignorance

In 2002, then U.S. Secretary of Defense Donald Rumsfeld was probably referencing a beautiful Persian poem by Ibn Yamin in a press conference when he made his (in)famous "known unknowns" remarks. The poem wrestles with knowledge and uncertainty. Mr. Rumsfeld was attempting to help people process the early days of the Iraq invasion and the uncertainty that came with it. The famous poem gives us a gift: a framework for living in an uncertain world.

Here is the poem, translated by theoretical physicist Niayesh Afshordi (2016):

One who knows and knows that he knows...
His horse of wisdom will reach the skies.

One who knows, but doesn't know that he knows...
He is fast asleep, so you should wake him up!

One who doesn't know, but knows that he doesn't know...
His limping mule will eventually get him home.

One who doesn't know and doesn't know that he doesn't know...
He will be eternally lost in his hopeless oblivion!

Knowledge and Action

One who knows and knows that he knows...
His horse of wisdom will reach the skies.

The straightforward side effects and pitfalls are the ones you know, understand, and act on to avoid or reduce harm. When you see bad and do something about it, your "horse of wisdom will reach the sky." Pay attention to known problems with AI that have solutions, and if you're motivated and able, be part of the solution.

Knowledge with Uncertainty

One who knows, but doesn't know that he knows...
He is fast asleep, so you should wake him up!

Harder are side effects and pitfalls you can see but not understand or know how to address. You know something bad is going to happen but not exactly how to do something about it. You are fast asleep, so you should wake up! Trust your instincts. If you think there is a problem with AI in your work or life, but don't know for sure, you're probably right. Follow the "see something, say something" rule. Bring it up, talk about it. Try not to catastrophize, rather to understand.

Knowledge with Your Head in the Sand

> *One who doesn't know, but knows that he doesn't know...*
> *His limping mule will eventually get him home.*

This is the head-in-the-sand or profits-before-principles category that is the most disturbing to me: Ignoring known risks in a mad dash for "creative destruction" by corporations and their leaders—the same Masters of the Universe who brought you the dot com crash, the 2008 financial crisis, and subsequent recessions. Mark Zuckerberg, knowing he'll be OK in the end, plows ahead despite the risks. "His limping mule will eventually get him home."

It's not just the Big AI "them," but increasingly also the leadership of every corporation or large nonprofit built on human knowledge work. Geoffrey Hinton is a canary in the coal mine, warning us that there is internal knowledge with external denial.

Your job is to ask the hard questions in the all-hands meeting, the school board meeting, or in the customer satisfaction survey.

Bring up solutions to go with known problems. Show leadership even if you're no AI expert.

Ignorance

> *One who doesn't know and doesn't know that he doesn't know...*
> *He will be eternally lost in his hopeless oblivion!*

There are unknown risks. Things we can't see, often because of groupthink. You're completely ignorant of what might happen. Worse, you aren't even aware of your ignorance. You're blind to what might happen and may have a false sense of security. With stakes as high as our world faces with AI, it's important to consider where we may have a blind spot.

Nassim Nicholas Taleb's book *The Black Swan* is helpful again in this context. Often, individuals will call out a risk that their group can't see. Pay attention to these lone voices, often seen as contrarian or disruptive. What can they tell you? Would it really cost that much to mitigate a seemingly unthinkable risk, considering the downside?

In conclusion, AI is brand new but has a lot of momentum behind it. Ibn Yamin's poem goes against our instinct, our drive to stay in our comfort zone of knowledge, to put our heads in the sand. Artificial intelligence brings much uncertainty and holds unseen challenges of which we are ignorant. The best defense is a good offense built on as much knowledge, understanding, and practice as we can pull off. Which brings you to the final chapter—using AI in your life!

References

Afshordi, Niayesh, 2016. *He Will Be Eternally Lost in His Hopeless Oblivion!* (Retrieved on April 24, 2025, from https://nafshordi.com/2016/07/26/he-will-be-eternally-lost-in-his-hopeless-oblivion/)

Fontana, Ash, & Mark Gorenberg, 2016. *Growing Up in the Intelligence Era.* TechCrunch. (Retrieved on May 9, 2025, from Growing up in the intelligence era | TechCrunch)

Gerkin, Tom, 2023. *New York Times Sues Microsoft and OpenAI for 'Billions.'* BBC. (Retrieved on May 2, 2025, from New York Times sues Microsoft and OpenAI for 'billions')

Kleinman, Zoe, & Chris Vallance, 2023. *AI 'Godfather' Geoffrey Hinton Warns of Dangers as He Quits Google.* BBC. (Retrieved on April 22, 2025, from AI 'godfather' Geoffrey Hinton warns of dangers as he quits Google)

Masanet, Eric, Arman Shehabi, Nuoa Lei, et al., 2020. *Recalibrating Global Data Center Energy-Use Estimates. Science* 367, 984–986. (Retrieved on April 24, 2025, from Recalibrating global data center energy-use estimates | Science)

Pope, Audrey, 2024. *NYT v. OpenAI: The Times's About-Face.* Harvard Law Review, April 10. (Accessed on May 14, 2025, from https://harvardlawreview.org/blog/2024/04/nyt-v-openai-the-timess-about-face/)

Rogelberg, Sasha, 2024. *Fashion Giant Shein Has Been Slapped with Yet Another Lawsuit Alleging Copyright Infringement, Data Scraping, and AI to Steal Art: 'It's Somewhat Shocking That They've Been Able to Get Away With It'* Fortune, April 16. (Retrieved on May 2, 2025, from Artists sue Shein, accusing it of using AI and data scraping to steal their art | Fortune)

Supreme Court of the United States, 2001. *New York Times Company, Inc., et al., Petitioners v. Jonathan Tasini et al.* (Retrieved on May 14, 2025, from https://www.law.cornell.edu/supct/pdf/00-

201P.ZO)

United Nations Office for Disarmament Affairs, 2023. Lethal Autonomous Weapon Systems (LAWS). (Retrieved on April 23, 2025, from https://disarmament.unoda.org/the-convention-on-certain-conventional-weapons/background-on-laws-in-the-ccw/)

CHAPTER 5:

Make AI Work for You (On Your Terms)

If you're a student or recent graduate, you're almost certain to be a regular user of AI. Believe it or not, you're among the only existing group of experts at using modern AI. If you're further along in your life and work, you're less likely to deliberately use AI. It's a tool you may use here and there for a specific task. You may do some experimenting, but it's most likely not yet a no-brainer, go-to resource.

Students, I'm jealous of you. Everyone else, I get it. I write this in my early fifties. Artificial intelligence is the first technological change in my lifetime to challenge my ability to adapt. When the personal computer became accessible, my parents were in their thirties and got one right away. I learned to use it at home after elementary school. I learned to type and use spreadsheets on a computer in my public middle school. When dial-up services came on the scene, I connected my PC to the first internet communities and chatted online in high school in the eighties and college in the early nineties. A few years after Tim Berners-Lee invented the World Wide Web in 1989, my friend Sam showed me a primitive website with pictures of ancient caves published by someone far away from our college. A few years after that, I worked at Ask Jeeves, an early web search company. When the cell phone became ubiquitous in the late nineties, I texted my friends last minute social plans, to the amazement of my parents' generation. When the smartphone came out in the mid-2000s, I started using one without thinking twice. But AI makes me feel the calcification of age. It's the first widespread technology in my lifetime that I just don't want to deal with. I'm fortunate to be an insider. It's my job to help my organization understand and use AI. I see so much potential to positively impact the world I live in and the world my grandchildren will live in. But it's really hard. Contrast my situation with that of my daughter who is experiencing the start of AI in the same way I experienced the dawn of the World Wide Web. ChatGPT arrived during her freshman year of college. Her brain and expectations were what neurologists call plastic—still moldable. She started using AI because she didn't know any different. It's been amazing to see how rapidly her methods of accomplishing her schoolwork have evolved.

My daughter is responding to AI under a new evolutionary pressure. We're used to thinking of evolution resulting from something "bad" happening. A comet striking the earth. Climate change. A new virus. Artificial intelligence is not that, though it may sometimes seem so. Artificial intelligence is like the printed book. The invention of moveable type was an evolutionary pressure that accelerated and widened the exit of civilization from the Middle Ages. Europe's Middle Ages were not romantic knights and princesses. Picture population decline, feudal subjugation of peasants, plague, famine and wars. One war lasted so long, it was called the Hundred Years War. It was so bad, that some historians referred to the whole mess as the Dark Ages. Europe got out of this civilizational decline because of printed books. More and more knowledge was captured in books. More and more people learned to read. People could contribute, could create value beyond their back-breaking manual labor, fighting ability, or birth. A kid who learned to read could grow up to do anything. People living in Europe through historical periods following the Middle Ages came to value book-enabled knowledge and education for pulling them out of their grandparents' and great-grandparents' desperate times, when the graves from the plague were still fresh. Books and education were so revolutionary in terms of human well-being, people in Europe and elsewhere established public libraries and schools to further share and democratize knowledge.

Let's jump into the future and rewrite that last passage:

> *"More and more knowledge was captured in AI. More and more people learned to use AI. People could contribute, could create value beyond their mind-numbing office labor, their access to expensive higher education, their network of rich friends. A kid who learned to use AI could grow up to do anything. People living through historical periods following the chaos and stagnation of postmodernity came to value AI-enabled knowledge and education for pulling them out of their parents' and grandparents' desperate times, when graves from the pandemics were still fresh. AI was so revolutionary in terms of human well-being, people established public large language models."*

I see AI as having the same potential to improve our fragile world as the book did hundreds of years ago. Enough to quit my job and write this book. Enough to creakily learn to use AI so I can respond to its evolutionary pressure just as my ancestors did with books. And it's both as simple and complex as that.

Use AI

The more we use AI in a thoughtful, informed way to improve the quality of our work and our lives, the better the long-term outcome for us as individuals and for our society. Like it or not, AI is an inevitable and inextricable part of our lives, just like all the revolutionary technological changes that came before: the printing press, the household telephone, the pocket camera, the personal computer, the World Wide Web, the smartphone, and social media—all of which became extraordinarily beneficial when put to creative use by billions of humans. All of which have their own side effects and pitfalls.

In every case, recognition of the costs, benefits, and creative use of the technology by people like you steered (or is steering) these industries to better human outcomes through user (consumer)-driven change. The same can happen with AI.

Where to start?

Augment Your Life

Start by answering three questions: What are you good at? What do you want to be better at? What do you need to do but takes an unsustainable amount of time or effort? If this feels like therapy, or is maybe a bit uncomfortable, you're not alone. Another word for augmentation is "self-improvement" or "self-help." It can be challenging to take a critical look at your life and how you live it and then try to make changes. It's even weirder to do that and then consider getting help from "artificial intelligence." But doing so can help you succeed, lead, and remain engaged in the modern era.

Let's take myself as an example. I'm good at coming up with creative ideas. I want to be better at doing my laundry regularly. I need to keep my email inbox clean, but it takes too much time.

We turn the tables on technology when we approach it with the goal of living a more satisfying life. My ultimate goal isn't to "use AI" any more than it is to "use a smartphone." My goal (and yours) should be to get more out of my natural efforts and abilities, enhance creativity, and pursue new and different projects that I might not be able to tackle on my own. How can AI be a means to this end? I'll go first.

I started a completely unrelated podcast as a creative outlet about a year before writing this book. While I was writing, my daughter and I started another podcast to share stories of living with AI, also called "You Teach The Machines." We figured that since this is all so new, lots of people are going to have new and different experiences with AI and it would be helpful for others to hear about them. A fun podcast needs music, so we made a theme song with a music generation AI. I wrote the lyrics and set a few other parameters, and in about an hour we were able to dress up our human discussion with machine-generated music. My creative contributions were the lyrics I wrote and the direction I gave the AI. Artificial intelligence helped me make more of my ideas by generating a catchy tune, along with vocals. It has turned out to be a hit with the college students we interview! Now, do I value this music as much as the original music I hired my friend, talented singer-songwriter Jay Nash to write, perform, and record for my other podcast? No. My collaboration with Jay led to a live performance on stage together and ongoing creative human collaboration. Did I create a fun little musical addition that enhances our AI podcast more than generic stock music? Yes! It's always fun to learn in areas where you're already familiar, so if you're new to AI, music is a great place to start.

Everyone is familiar with washing dirty clothes. We have to do it; we don't want to do it. I want to be better doing my laundry regularly. My clothes build up on both the dirty and clean side of the washing machine cycle. My hamper is always full of two to three loads, which creates an artificial mental block in and of itself. I feel great when I manage to run it all, fold it, and reflect confidently on a two-week supply of clean underwear. But that's not happening regularly. So what's a way that AI could help? (Besides a laundry robot—we're not there yet, and, to be honest, the waiter robots I saw in a dim sum restaurant in Chicago were both creepy and entertaining, but I can't imagine having one in my house.)

We'll start with the ground rule that the machine isn't going to do my laundry for me. A simple use of AI to improve my laundry habits is to use tools for behavior or habit change. I asked both my smart speaker and the digital assistant on my phone to set weekly reminders to start a load of laundry on Thursday evening, switch to the dryer Friday morning, and prompt me to fold on Friday evening. You may already be doing something similar in your life. Guess what? It worked!

Gentle reminders are a good start, but what if I had less laundry in the first place? I enlisted AI to reduce the amount of laundry I have by finding clothing that doesn't require as frequent washing. Retailers have been working on AI-enabled wardrobe recommendations since the dawn of e-commerce. In fact, a social media algorithm recently profiled me as an "outfit repeater" as it served me an ad for odor- and stain-resistant pants. We didn't call Jeeves "AI" when I worked as a software engineer at Ask Jeeves. That term was out of vogue, redolent of mid-century science fiction. Instead, we called Jeeves "Natural Language Understanding," the marketing term for natural language processing, which we defined in Chapter One. We built a wardrobe recommendation search engine so Jeeves could pick out a Gap or Nike outfit like a proper digital butler. Fast forward twenty-five years and I can try using any number of free AI-enabled personal clothing assistants "who" will set me up with an entire wardrobe of outfits I can "repeat." In fact, I did just that while writing this book! There are a bunch of clothing recommendation apps available on your smartphone.

What don't I have time for but need to get done? This one is straightforward and probably something you're already benefitting from anyway. Go into your email account and look for your spam or junk folder. Open it and witness the result of teaching a machine to do beneficial work. We discussed this in a previous chapter, but it's worth revisiting. Spam email is a fact of life. Artificial intelligence controls spam. You couldn't pay me enough to filter spam out of my inbox. I'm very grateful for the AI that does it for me.

Now It's Your Turn

Start by answering these three questions for yourself:

- What am I good at?
- What do I want to be better at?
- What do I have to do but life gets in the way?

Try not to overthink it; just write down whatever comes to mind for each. Now go through the exercise of looking for ways to augment your life using AI for each question. If you get stuck, it may well be that there isn't a ready answer—yet! If that's the case, consider what you would want from an AI tool and be on the lookout.

If you find an option that seems helpful, remember to always evaluate the AI using what you've learned in the previous chapters. You are an informed user and consumer of AI, and you are capable of making a decision to use it or not depending on your own viewpoint.

It's important to step back and focus on your humanity now that you've considered AI in your life. The most important thing you can do is recognize what makes you uniquely human. You don't want to be a machine. You'll never compete successfully with a machine. So don't try, and instead focus on your human abilities. That's the point of a wonderful book called *Futureproof: 9 Rules for Humans in the Age of Automation*, by Kevin Roose. Here's an example. My friend Jean is an architect with a thriving independent practice. Another architect I know, David, is getting out of the business after seeing his income erode. David is incredibly technically proficient. His eye for design, proportion, and ability to model is top notch, but he's not so great with people. Jean is an excellent designer, but maybe not as good as David. What Jean has is empathy, patience, and an understanding of how to help her clients navigate the rocky emotional and financial experience of designing and building something as personal as a home. Jean brings her humanity to bear on her business. She has what some call emotional intelligence, and importantly, the ability to use it in her work. David, not so much. David and Jean are already subject to the pressures of automation. AI-enabled architecture design software is becoming ubiquitous. I'm not worried about Jean in the coming years, but David is smart to seek alternatives.

Augmentation shouldn't be about becoming a cyborg. *Futureproof* is a great read because it illustrates that if you just use machines to hustle harder, work faster, you'll eventually be replaced by a robot. Augmentation should be about helping yourself be more human, doing more of the things humans can do. Cyborgs and Terminators are creepy because they are machines pretending to be humans. When we use AI to try to make ourselves more machine-like, we're creepy too. Use AI to be more human, not the other way around. Reading *Futureproof* can help you understand your uniquely human qualities in a world of increasing automation. It's an important book because it can help you develop a defensive strategy for the change AI is bringing. Help you differentiate yourself by strengthening your best human qualities. In this book, I strive to present an optimistic offensive strategy. I hope to help you build on the message of *Futureproof* and use AI so you can make informed choices, influence how AI develops, have more fun, and have an even greater impact on the world around you.

Using AI for Personal Safety

My mutt dog, Lilo, is a perfect example of specialized, superhuman intelligence in action. She lies dormant on the couch or bed until her sensors detect something of concern. It could be footsteps on the driveway, the scent of a fox approaching our duck coop, or the sleepwalking of one of my children. I will never surpass her ability to hear, smell, or intuit. I will never beat her vigilant cognitive processing that detects and responds to concerns at all hours, day and night. Even while in a deep sleep, upside down, looking ridiculous, she will lift a head, cock an ear, sniff the air to gather more information. She growls a warning above a certain threshold. When a threat is confirmed, she loses her mind, barking and scratching at the door to defend her humans from possible harm. If I were allergic to dogs, I would want a machine or alarm system that could do all of this for me.

Safety concerns present humans with one of the greatest opportunities to benefit from AI. A machine can be taught to be ever vigilant and to detect possible harm before we can. Machines can learn from our environment what is "normal" and what may be something to worry about. A machine can learn that the mail is delivered every afternoon. Which, apparently, my dogs can't do because they attempt to murder our mailman, Bill, every day at two-thirty in the afternoon, even though he leaves them dog biscuits.

Safety-critical situations are a great place to take advantage of AI. You're building layers of redundancy by adding a machine into your life to keep you safer. In my own life, I have seen major safety benefits from the AI in my car.

Imagine Lilo perched on the dash of my car. She stares intently through the windshield, never blinking. I put the car in reverse to back out of the driveway and she runs to the back of the car, furiously scanning through one hundred and eighty degrees for any hazard. She barks at the sight of a pedestrian walking into the path of the car, out of my line of sight but visible to Lilo's well-trained eyes. I brake and the pedestrian strolls safely by (hopefully without a dog of their own so I don't end up with the two knuckleheads barking uncontrollably in the car).

The good news is you don't have to train a dog to be your safe-driving assistant. Most new cars now include AI systems that do even more to keep you safe on the road. As we discussed in chapters 1 and 2, these systems are trained to recognize a bunch of hazards through cameras, radar, and driver inputs to the steering wheel. Some even watch your eyes and can detect when you're getting sleepy. Every time you drive a car with one of these systems, you're putting the machine through continuing education. The car records and uploads data about the safety system to the manufacturer to help improve the AI (and probably sell your data to Starbucks so they can decide where to put a new store, but let's focus on the positives). Driving safety is a very positive outcome from all of us collectively teaching machines.

I know I'm a safer driver in my reasonably priced 2024 Subaru that came standard with Advanced Driver Assistance Systems (ADAS). My ADAS has prevented at least two collisions where I absolutely would have rear-ended another driver. In both cases, it detected a car coming to a sudden stop in front of me and slammed on the brakes just before I did. The machine saved me from an expensive inconvenience at best, and from hurting another driver and myself at worst. When our teenage drivers go on long trips, this is the car they take. My wife's and my criterion for a kid's car used to be the cheapest car with air bags and a top crash safety rating. Now, when we can afford it, we help them replace their old beaters with cars running AI safety systems. Never going back!

This safety feature also helps my dad drive safely at night now that he's lost vision in one of his eyes. When he got his first car with an AI safety system, his stress levels dropped from knowing that everyone would be safer when he had to drive my mom to the hospital or come home from a concert after dark. I am a car enthusiast and truly enjoy the raw driving experience. I own and drive three classic vehicles (1982 Jeep CJ5, 1982 GMC C6000, 1995 Toyota Tacoma) that don't even have airbags, much less sensors and AI safety systems. Warning beeps and robots making decisions for me seemed like an intrusion into a meditative escape. That can be true, but the value of these systems is so clear, I now do ninety-nine percent of my driving in the Subaru with the help of AI. AI can really, truly improve our safety, the safety of our loved ones, and the well-being of people with whom we share the road.

Be a Smarter Patient

The potential for AI to help us be healthy, or at least less unhealthy, is remarkable. If AI captures human knowledge and makes it accessible at scale, then the knowledge of clinicians could have a great impact through its careful use. The health industry is an enormous, nearly $20 trillion-with-a-T sector of the American economy. Venture capitalists are already investing in AI startups and directly in the sector and are certain to invest more with that much money at stake. The typical economics of health mean that investment follows the money, as has been the case in the pharmaceutical and medical device industries. In my work, the earliest adoption of AI is in hospital financial operations—billing, collection of unpaid bills, and pre-approval and increased approval of insurance claims. These are all worthwhile efforts to gain incremental efficiency in the complex financial enterprise of a large hospital. After financial operations, AI is being used to sustain or increase the margin of already (relatively) high-margin treatment and diagnostic care. In both cases, investment follows returns. But there is so much more potential.

So how is a patient to profit from AI? First, try to avoid being a patient. Health screening is an excellent area for the use of AI. At a minimum, when it's time for your colonoscopy, you can look for a gastroenterologist who also uses GI Genius or another computerized adenoma detection tool. Ask them how it has affected their adenoma detection rate. It's a good sign if they have a concrete answer. For other types of screening, get a sense of the growing number of health AI systems approved by the Food and Drug Administration (FDA), listed on their website (https://www.fda.gov/medical-devices/software-medical-device-samd/artificial-intelligence-and-machine-learning-aiml-enabled-medical-devices at the time of publication). More than one thousand had been approved at the time this book was written.

Ask your doctor, nurse, or hospital administrator what they're doing to evaluate and adopt AI systems that improve the care they provide. You may be surprised at their answer. Ask them how they are paying for the system so you can evaluate how their incentives align with your own health needs. Ask them how they have ensured the AI will perform fairly for all patients. Ask them how they are checking the performance of AI over time to make sure it continues to perform.

Cornucopia

What follows is a collection of real stories from people just like you who have tried using AI. Consider these stories encouragement to try AI for the same use, or for a different but related use. Ask yourself what aspects of the story could translate to your own life or work. Get in the habit of asking people you know how they are using AI. You may be surprised at their creative problem solving.

Awesome Editor

Ann, the developmental editor of this book, used AI for the first time to edit the Introduction. She started by editing the raw draft manually, using her laptop and Microsoft Word. This gave her a version she was happy with as the product of her decades of expertise. She then went back to the raw draft and fed it into an AI service, asking the AI to edit it for clarity and enhance it for content. We then sat down together and compared the two results, one entirely manual by a human expert, one done by an AI. We found that Ann made edits the AI did not that were important to me, the author. She had acquired a sense of my "voice" through our multiple meetings to develop an outline and her subsequent reading and editing of my draft. Her editing helped bring my voice out and make it stronger in the written words of the Introduction. Watch a singer with their vocal coach and you'll see the coach help the singer find more expressive, impactful vocalizations of the sounds they are creating. That's what Ann does for me. In comparison, the AI is like the auto-tuner used by recording studios and pop musicians to polish and make vocals appealing. You hear about "heavy" versus "light" use of the auto-tuner. The Introduction we got back from the AI was like the auto-tuner turned up to eleven. Technically my words and ideas, so very polished, but no longer… me. The AI-edited Introduction appears in the Appendix, along with the prompts we used to generate it. Decide for yourself which is "better."

Japanese Dinner

My friend Rob used AI to teach himself to put a seven-course meal on the table while everything was hot. Rob loves to try new things in the kitchen. He recently started learning traditional Japanese ingredients and recipes, cooking one dish at a time using cookbooks, videos, and online information. After getting familiar with a bunch of dishes, he wanted to do something special for family and friends and cook a multi-course meal. The problem was that it was really hard to learn how to time the preparation and cooking of a wide variety of dishes so they would all come to the table hot at the same time. He asked an AI for the ordered series of steps required to prepare, plate, and serve all seven recipes. He followed the composite recipe and succeeded at serving a hot seven-course meal the first time he tried.

Memorial Podcast

My friend Diane wrote a memorial message at the passing of her mother. She read it aloud to friends and loved ones at her mother's funeral, sharing a warm remembrance of a life well-lived. A number of people who could not be there heard about Diane's message and asked for a recording of her reading, which didn't exist. Uncomfortable with making a standalone recording, she decided to try an AI service typically used to create audio podcasts from written information. The resulting podcast had two perfect-sounding human voices sharing Diane's written message as a warm conversational tribute to her mother. She sent the audio to far-away friends and family, who took grateful comfort from the tribute.

Wholesale Metal

My friend Johan uses AI to read metal supplier specification documents from hundreds of suppliers to his wholesale metal business. He works with many suppliers to build and maintain a diverse inventory of products from space-age alloy tubes for building airplanes to rough steel stakes for farming tomatoes. Each supplier sends an electronic copy of a document describing the metal product, lot, and batch information along with the actual metal products on a truck. That information needs to be transferred into Johan's inventory and sales database. It's challenging because every supplier uses their own document format. Stock-keeping unit, description, batch number, lot number, and safety information all appear on every document, but in slightly different places. He used optical character recognition (OCR) software for years to partially "read" the documents, with limited success. Recently, he started experimenting with AI systems that have been taught to retrieve information from different parts of documents based on a prompt such as "give me a list of all stock-keeping unit identifiers along with the accompanying description." He hopes this tool will help improve the quality and timeliness of inventory and sales information so his sales team can sell more and his warehouse team can fill more orders.

Robotic Coffee Machines

My friend Stephan uses AI to help his coffee machine customers troubleshoot problems in faraway places. He cofounded and leads Poursteady, a robotic pour-over coffee machine company. But these coffee machines are global. Poursteady machines are installed in coffee shops as far away as Korea and the Middle East, meaning that when a customer needs help, it could be the middle of the night in Brooklyn. He subscribed to an AI service that "read" all of the technical and how-to documentation and the ten years of customer-support emails Poursteady had collected. This was an example of fine-tuning a pre-existing generic foundation AI so it can help with coffee machines. The result is an AI chat "bot" that can answer questions and help troubleshoot problems based on its prior knowledge of the world (from the foundation AI model) and what it has learned about Poursteady's products (the fine-tuned AI). His staff further teaches the AI by asking it for help based on their expert knowledge of what has gone wrong in the past and confirming or correcting its answers (something you do when you use ChatGPT). With a well-taught machine in hand, his team hopes to give it to their distributors in Korea and the Middle East so they can better use the knowledge captured from Poursteady experts in Brooklyn. The economics of Stephan's young business are such that he can afford to either manufacture his coffee machines in Brooklyn or hire humans to do twenty-four-hour customer support, but not both. He is choosing to manufacture in the U.S. and scale the customer support knowledge of his expert team with the help of AI.

Boat Influencer

Dockdeals is an Instagram account run by an anonymous boat enthusiast who uses AI to quickly create high-quality visuals for boat-for-sale listings he is excited about. He uses a service called Canva to process low-quality pictures from the for-sale listing into high-quality images that jump out and better represent what he thinks is cool about the boats. He learned that Instagram's algorithm favors high-quality pictures and will show his posts to more people if he uses AI to improve the images.

Team Builder

My friend Jason runs a consulting company that uses AI to put together the best possible teams. His company builds financial analysis tools for businesses all over the world. Projects are successful when one or two of his analysis tool experts work as a team with one or two financial experts from the business. He subscribed to a service that uses an AI model to match people into high functioning teams or at least identify possible personality conflicts to be on the lookout for and work to avoid. He used the AI service with a few projects and found that it had helpful suggestions that improved the performance and satisfaction of the teams.

Insurance Appeals

A former colleague used early AI to automatically appeal denied insurance claims and pre-approvals to pay for prenatal diagnostic testing. This system overwhelmed the insurance companies, who then came to the table to negotiate blanket approvals. In my experience, insurance companies deny and delay payment in the hope of creating disincentives that reduce the rate at which they pay claims, likely with the help of AI. In this case, my colleague fought fire with fire and used AI to level the playing field.

Financial Reporting

A friend uses AI to analyze and generate summaries of why financial results change from quarter to quarter for the divisions of a holding company. Every division—and there are many—is required to explain why their sales, expenses, and profits are up or down. The head of the division provides a narrative explanation, really the only way to analyze and capture the complexity of the situation. In addition to human analysis, they use AI to read all the explanations, identify unique events, find possible trends, and generate summary explanations across an incredibly complex array of subsidiary businesses.

Search

My godson uses ChatGPT instead of Google for all his web searches. He was in his freshman year of college when ChatGPT was released. He started playing around with it early on. When I heard he bought a paid subscription to ChatGPT, I felt it said a lot about the utility he found in the tool. On top of not having much money because he's a full-time student, he's also frugal in the nicest possible way. Generous to others, but it pains him to waste money. He uses ChatGPT constantly to look up information and identify trees and buildings from pictures he takes with his phone.

Study Aid

My daughter used AI to generate practice problems while studying for a final exam. She struggled with a class in college one recent semester. It was a requirement for her major, and she needed a C or above. There was a real possibility of a D or worse! It wasn't enough to go to all of the professor's office hours, seek help from the teaching assistant, study with classmates. She prompted AI by asking it to generate practice problems for concepts in the lecture that hadn't been covered in prior homework assignments.

Retail

An engineer I interviewed for a job on my team used AI to help convenience store retailers stock their shelves to maximize sales-per-square-foot. The next time you go into a large chain convenience store, look up at the ceiling for dark plastic bubbles. You're right that these are for security to detect and prevent shoplifting, but if the store is a customer of my candidate's company, they do more. The convenience store AI has been taught to watch how individual people move through the store, browse shelves, choose items, and make purchases. After a few weeks of watching customers, it recommends changes to the store layout and to where products are displayed. The process continues after the changes are made, in a constant cycle of optimization and adaptation to changing customer behavior. Grocery stores are increasingly using this technology as well. Next time you notice that your favorite candy bar or bag of chips has moved to a new location, it's because AI thinks it'll sell better there.

I could go on, but in the end the best way for you to learn about AI is to use it. Hopefully, the variety of these stories can help you see how AI could be useful to you. AI is changing and evolving so rapidly that it's not feasible to write a definitive "how to" instruction manual. Also, the best AI should be easy to pick up and learn. With the information in this book, you now understand the fundamentals of how you and people like you teach machines and can choose how you engage with AI on your own terms. You are better equipped to recognize AI in the world around you, and with a healthy awareness of the current AI industry, you're a more knowledgeable consumer. Use your knowledge to influence how you live with AI by voting with your feet and wallet. You are better positioned to see the value of your data and decisions and to help your own school, business, or employer maximize the value of both in the use of AI.

Keep Up!

I started a podcast with my twenty-something daughter, Maryjane, so I can keep up with the evolution of AI in the real world—more how it's impacting people's lives as they use it, less the evolution of the underlying technology. We talk to students, educators, and experts about their life with AI. It's called "You Teach the Machines" and you can find it wherever you get your podcasts.

We started the podcast because this book is simultaneously the best way to share a holistic view of AI and the worst way to keep up with the constant change happening at the time you're reading or listening to it. Artificial intelligence evolved significantly in the time it took to write and publish this book. When I started writing in November of 2024, the latest available language AI were capable of responding to your prompt or question with a single answer. Four months later, the latest available AI was able to respond with an answer backed up by *the steps it took to figure out the answer!* It shared its reasoning! As an insider, this was both hugely necessary and mind-blowing.

The steady and rapid pace of change will continue, punctuated by Black Swan events. My hope is that by reading this book you shed uncertainty about AI and the fear it can cause. I hope that any remaining fear of the Five D's (Destruction, Deception, Dumbing Down, Disconnection, and Displacement) are rational and help you make better decisions. I hope you are better able to recognize your own Survival Signals when bad actors in the AI industry try to manipulate you in their marketing, and that you choose to support the AI companies that take the high road. I hope you are better equipped to manage unexpected change brought by future Black Swans. I hope you are better able to think critically about side effects and pitfalls of AI and, as a more informed consumer, can make choices consistent with your values. I hope you have a new appreciation for the incredible value of your data and the data you generate—truly how you teach the machines—and exert more influence over how it is used. Most of all, I hope you see AI for the incredibly useful tool it can be when it augments your life. I encourage you to seek out AI and experiment with it in your life and work. Be the windshield, not the bug. You teach the machines!

References

Roose, Kevin, 2021. *Futureproof: 9 Rules for Humans in the Age of Automation.* Random House.

U.S. Food and Drug Administration, 2025. *Artificial Intelligence and Machine Learning (AI/ML)–Enabled Medical Devices.* (Retrieved on May 10, 2025, from https://www.fda.gov/medical-devices/software-medical-device-samd/artificial-intelligence-and-machine-learning-aiml-enabled-medical-devices)

Appendix

Transcript of editing the first draft of the introduction to this book using ChatGPT running GPT-4o on May 14, 2025. Note that at the time the book was titled *We Teach the Machines*. Author's prompts are in plain text, AI response in ***italics***:

Please edit the following for clarity, accuracy and add additional detail where it would be helpful for a lay reader.

> ***Sure, please provide the text you'd like me to edit. Once I have it, I'll revise it for clarity, accuracy, and add helpful details for a lay audience.***

Introduction

Large Language Model. GenAI. Generative. Training. ChatGPT. Hallucination. Explainability. Machine Learning. Neural Network. Deep Learning. Natural Language Processing.

These words are synonymous with Artificial Intelligence (AI). AI is what we call computer systems we teach to do (hopefully beneficial) work. Sometimes we teach machines to find patterns of information we humans can't in big collections of data. Like the relationship between all possible English sentences and all possible German sentences. Sometimes we teach machines to do a general task in a way that augments our lives. Like translate any English you give it to German.

You've picked up this book because suddenly "AI" seemingly comes up in every conversation and work meeting, shows up in every search…

[remainder of original draft intentionally left out for brevity.]

[The following is the AI response:]

This is a strong and engaging introduction—conversational, rich in historical parallels, and packed with relatable context. A few suggestions to refine and strengthen it:

Strengths

1. **Historical Framing**: Drawing parallels to writing and printing is highly effective. It gives readers context and a sense of continuity.

2. **Tone and Accessibility**: The informal, friendly tone with moments of humor makes complex material approachable.

3. **Clear Purpose**: The promise to demystify AI and empower readers is compelling.

Suggestions for Improvement

1. **Structure and Pacing**

* **Break Up Long Paragraphs**: Some sections are dense. Consider breaking them into smaller chunks to improve readability, especially for a general audience.

* **Use Subheadings**: You could add thematic subheadings (e.g., "From Cuneiform to Chatbots," "The Gutenberg Effect," "The Black Swan Moment") to help guide readers through the narrative.

2. **Clarify and Focus Key Points**

* **Refine the Central Analogy**: You compare AI to both writing and printing—consider being a bit more precise. Is AI more like the invention of writing (a new way to preserve knowledge) or more like the printing

press (a new way to scale access)?

** **Tighten Tangents**: For instance, the story about Gutenberg's business being taken over is fascinating but could be condensed to maintain momentum.*

*#### 3. **Tone and Style Adjustments***

** Some phrases feel slightly informal or ambiguous for a published introduction (e.g., "witchcraft," "unwashed general public," "creepily good"). Consider whether a slightly more neutral or respectful tone would be appropriate depending on your target audience.*

** Instead of "\[Washington Post article]" or "\[REF]," insert placeholder citations you plan to complete later or add a note like "(citation needed)" if still pending.*

*#### 4. **Clarify Key Definitions Early***

** Consider introducing and defining "Large Language Model," "Generative AI," and "Neural Network" earlier—perhaps even in a sidebar or a glossary if you plan to use them often.*

*#### 5. **Reinforce Your Unique Framing***

** The "We Teach the Machines" framing is powerful. Bring it back at the end of the introduction to frame what's coming next. E.g., "This book will show you how we, collectively and individually, teach the machines—and how we can do it more wisely.*

Would you like help polishing this into a clean, publish-ready introduction or assistance with outlining/structuring upcoming chapters?

Yes, please polish this into a clean, publish-ready introduction.

Absolutely. Below is a polished version of your

introduction, maintaining your voice, intent, and core ideas, while improving flow, clarity, and tone for a general audience.

Introduction: We Teach the Machines

In the history of human communication, two inventions changed everything.

The first was writing. Before writing, knowledge lived only in people's minds, passed down orally and often lost or distorted over time. Writing allowed us to record ideas, transmit them across distances, and preserve them for future generations. It was revolutionary—but it was also exclusive. For most of history, reading and writing were reserved for the elite: priests, scribes, kings. Knowledge was power, and power was kept tightly controlled.

The second was the printing press. When Johannes Gutenberg mechanized the process of reproducing written words in the 15th century, everything changed again. Suddenly, ideas could spread faster and farther than ever before. Literacy rates soared. Scientific knowledge, political theory, religious reform—all exploded across Europe. The world shifted from the age of scribes to the age of readers. Information became democratized. The press reshaped society.

Now, we're living through a third revolution—one that, like the printing press, is transforming how we communicate, learn, and create. This time, the invention is artificial intelligence.

More specifically, it's the rise of systems like ChatGPT—technologies powered by Large Language Models (LLMs) that can understand and generate human language with startling fluency. These systems can answer questions, write essays, translate languages, generate code, summarize complex documents, and even create poetry or fiction. They seem intelligent. They seem creative. Sometimes, they even seem human.

But they are not human. And they are not magic.

They are machines. Machines that learn from us.

This is the central idea of the book you're holding: **we teach the machines**.

Not in a metaphorical sense. Quite literally, the way these systems "learn" is by absorbing the words we've written—on the internet, in books, in transcripts, in code repositories. They process patterns in language based on the data we feed them. When you talk to an AI, you're talking to a reflection of us: of everything we've written, said, and shared.

That means we—individually and collectively—shape what these machines know, what they say, and how they behave.

And that gives us power.

You don't need a computer science degree to understand what's happening. You don't need to be a tech insider or an AI engineer. You just need to understand the basics of how these systems work, what their limitations are, and how your everyday interactions help to shape them.

That's what this book is about. It's not a technical manual, and it's not a manifesto. It's a guide—a practical, clear-eyed look at how we got here, how this technology works, and what it means for you, your work, your creativity, and your future.

Because whether you're using AI tools today or not, they're becoming part of the infrastructure of daily life—like the internet, like smartphones, like writing itself. And just like past revolutions in communication, the people who understand the change are better *positioned to navigate it, shape it, and benefit from it.*

This book will give you that understanding.

It will also show you something deeper: that these systems are not just about machines getting smarter. They are about us—what we value, what we teach, what we choose to share. AI doesn't just reflect intelligence; it reflects culture, bias, beauty, cruelty, curiosity, and humor. It reflects humanity.

So let's demystify it. Let's get curious. Let's explore how we're teaching the machines—and how we can do it more wisely.

Welcome.

Your Notes

Your Notes

Acknowledgments:

A team of wonderful people worked with me to create *You Teach the Machines*. My developmental editor, Ann Campbell, coached me on how to start and finish the manuscript and made it so much better every time she touched it. The librarians at the Bala Cynwyd and Gladwyne Public Libraries assisted with research and welcomed me every winter morning. The entire team at Compass Rose Publishing showed great care in editing and production. Byron O'Neill designed the cover with enthusiasm, creativity, and patient professionalism. Special thanks to the early readers who spent time reading and providing critical feedback: Melissa Pennington, Katherine Pennington, John C. Pickford, Wendy Whittington, Jeffrey Miller, Philip Ketonis, and Panos Ketonis. You made the book better, and I am forever grateful.

Author Bio

Jeff Pennington has worked for more than twenty-five years in data, data science, and artificial intelligence. He has authored or co-authored more than twenty peer-reviewed papers in the fields of biomedical informatics and data privacy. Jeff started his career developing web search analytics at Ask Jeeves, the first major commercial natural language search engine. Most recently, Jeff led data and artificial intelligence as Chief Research Informatics Officer for the Children's Hospital of Philadelphia Research Institute where he worked for seventeen years before writing his first book. Jeff holds a bachelor's degree in biology and a master's degree in computer science.

Many thanks to you, the readers of,

YOU TEACH THE MACHINES.

Please ask for it

at your local library

or bookstore.

Reviews on

Amazon or Goodreads

are greatly appreciated.

Check out my podcast ***You Teach The Machines*** wherever you get your podcasts

Follow me on

LinkedIn

https://www.linkedin.com/in/penningtonjeff/

and

INSTAGRAM

@penningtonjeff

Check out my website at

www.youteachthemachines.com

For corporate, community, library or book club events.

Email: penningtonjeff@yahoo.com

www.ingramcontent.com/pod-product-compliance
Lightning Source LLC
LaVergne TN
LVHW022206200926
848481LV00006B/1870